MEDICINAL PLANTS OF TEXAS

NICOLE TELKES

Published in 2014 by Wildflower School of Botanical Medicine Publishing

PO BOX 337 Cedar Creek TX 78612 (412)294-8241
www.wildflowerherbschool.com

2nd Edition

ISBN-13: 9780615767567
BISAC: Nature / Plants / General

This book is dedicated to all of my teachers, students, my family, and my friends who have stuck by me as I wandered off the beaten path. Most of all I dedicate this to my husband, Jim, who wanders with me.

To you my dear reader, may you find more and more amazing plants to honor and enjoy!

CONTENTS

PREFACE

I wrote this book because Texas needed its own guide for medicinal plants. Like many others, I had gone into a local bookseller in Austin to find something on herbal medicine of Central Texas. What I found barely dipped into the flora we have or didn't take into account the differing bioregions and climates.

Much seemed to be written by people who studied plants, but not necessarily people who had used medicinal plants in practice. I spent the next fifteen years collecting every field guide I could for Central Texas and every book on anything that had to do with the plants of Texas.

On top of gathering books, I have been studying native and medicinal plants in the field and clinic, both in and out of Texas, compiling information on local plants, and testing plants on various ailments. Texas herbalism became a passion of mine. I work as a natural health practitioner using mainly herbs and bodywork to bring about balance in the body, and Texas herbs are a primary source of that balance. I formed the Wildflower School of Botanical Medicine in 2005 as a way to formalize the study of bioregional medicinal plants and help others connect to the bioregion they are living in.

I have learned that the study of local herbs is going to be a lifelong process, but after many exciting results, I decided it was time that a beginners' book should go out.

My interest in herbalism came from my work and love for nature. As a child I spent my summers exploring the forests of Northern Ontario and found my interest in ecology and plants continue into college. I attended the University of Texas asking to study herbal medicine and was told the closest I would get was environmental resource management in geography. So I entered into geography, minoring in botany. After graduating I got rid of all my possessions and went into direct action for social change, sitting in for old growth trees and blockading roads to protect wildlands. From those experiences I met politically savvy herbalists who took me deep into wild places and taught me about plants. By 1998, I had dedicated my life's work to the Green Path and to practicing as an herbalist. My main goal is to connect the health of the individual to the health of the environment. I thank all of my teachers, human and not, who influenced and inspired my work, and I hope to continue it for many years to come.

This book is here to empower you and as a gentle reminder that the answers to your questions about the local environment and your own health may be as close as your next door neighbor or the nearest empty ditch. Please go out and learn the plants of your region and the people of your region that specialize in holistic health. Everything you need to stay healthy is in front of you.

How to Use This Book

This book is a first edition and is meant to be used in conjunction with field guides or people who can properly identify plants. This book summarizes basic uses of plants and gives a general idea of what the plant looks like, but is more of a *materia medica* than a field guide. A field guide (of which Texas has many) focuses on how to identify the plant, not what it is used for. Since we have many good ones, I have chosen to focus in this book on how to use the plant instead. Please check the PDF resources accompanying this book for pictures and further study.

I offer this book to help people connect regionally with their natural world, in a philosophy of "locavorism" or what is called bioregionalism. I think it is essential that we form bonds and relationships with the plants and animals of our area of the country in order to preserve and protect our natural resources. Herbal medicine is the people's medicine. It is popular, working knowledge that we all must keep alive. The real knowledge does not come from books but from experience. My goal, and the goal of my school, is to have an herbalist on every corner!

Standard Disclaimer

This book is for informational purposes only and does not substitute for a trained medical practitioner. Information in this book is not meant to diagnose, prescribe, or treat any medical condition.

Special Acknowledgements:

This book took lots of helpful people to make it happen. I cannot possibly list everyone, but special thanks to my editors Isabel Stewart and Katie Walsh, and everyone who offered their photos for use. A full list of photo credits is available in the associated Photobook

A BIOREGIONAL LOOK AT TEXAS
CLIMATE, SEASONS, AND PLANTS

Texas doesn't seem to fit into any one bioregion; its land mass is far too large. We are not the Southwest or the Deep South or the Midwest. We are something like Occupied Mexico with a little bit of the other bioregions of the U.S. dipping in.

We encompass what used to be vast prairie and grasslands, filled with scrub and chaparral. From the southeast we receive climatic influences from the Gulf Coast, swamps, and bayou. From the northeast our plant communities are somewhat shaped by the Ozarks. From the west come tall mountains and rolling plains. Our biggest challenge is water, or not enough of it. You can get as detailed or general as you wish when describing the traits of Texas. For the purposes of this book, I am going to stay general.

Climate

Some of the biggest variables affecting when a plant blooms or is prolific are temperature, sun, and rainfall; and if you are in West Texas, elevation will also play a factor. A less commonly considered influence on plants is the "heat island" effect that cities have, especially here with the massive areas of concrete soaking up the solar rays and creating even hotter hot spots. The urban heat islands mean that plants may bloom a little earlier or not freeze back like they would outside of town.

Dry years may make for very short springs, late freezes may kill off our peaches and other flowering fruits, and if we get a mild enough early winter, sometimes the plants think it is a second false spring and the trees may put out buds, which rarely lead to fruit.

Mild winters can lead to biennial plants that usually live two years becoming perennial and living multiple years. This all lends to a pretty confusing time for many, trying to figure out actual delineations between seasons, what plants come out when, when the best time to pick is, and when the best time to plant is.

This book will mention the best time to harvest plant material based on my personal experience, but with all this said, it also depends on our seasonal influences that year. Many may have had other experiences. The plants in this book include invasive weeds and garden herbs, as well as more fragile natives.

Seasons

The first thing to remember is that most of Texas is not a temperate zone. In other words, for many parts of the state, gone is the idea of the four temperate zone seasons of spring, summer, winter, and fall. The further you go south, the more this is true. The people, the plants, the seasons—they all just kind of like to do their own thing.

We have cooler, wetter, greener times, and hotter, drier, browner times. Droughts are getting more extreme with climate change, and I wonder if we can stop just hoping to be out of them and figu-re out how to adapt, because as the years go on, even in my short time here, gardening and foraging has changed. The old rules do not apply, and living with drought has become the norm.

I don't think many of the rules that apply to northern climates (temperate zones) really apply down here when it comes to planting or picking your plants. Because our seasons are so variable, we don't fit many of the traditional gardening or harvesting guidelines of most herbals.

I feel bad for folks who pick up medicinal plant books from more temperate areas than ours, which say that you will find things like chickweed (*Stellaria media*) growing in the autumn. No, not in

9

most parts of Texas. For us, a plant like that would start up in winter to early spring and die back with the heat by about May.

Let's look at what I call "seasonish" influences, and note that this is coming from living in Central Texas.

"Seasonish" Influences

The seasonish influences include: spring, sprunner, summer, sumautumn, autumn, and winterish.

Spring

The cycle begins. Warmth returns with early springish weather.

Spring starts sometime in March and is mostly delineated by when our last freeze is and how much water we receive. Whispers of warmth arriving back to us in Central Texas are apparent in the flowers of winter: anemones turning to seed, the perfume of agarita along greenbelts attracting sleepy bees to them, and the bright violet-to-pink spiderwort blooms appearing.

Annual nettles make their appearance with corydalis in the greenbelts. Greenbrier puts out tiny little leaves that taste so good. Our redbud trees burst into a riot of vitamin C–rich pink flowers, and toxic mountain laurel shrubs unfurl grape bubblegum–scented flower arrangements, followed by fields of wildflowers beginning to show their colors by late March to early April.

I tend to think of the wildflowers coming in two waves. The early wave in spring consists of evening primrose, prairie vervain, bluebonnets, and paintbrushes starting late March and ending by May. We plant all of our annual, warm season veggies and watch our gardens fill with poppies, borage, calendula, and cilantro blooms. The air is still cool and crisp, the bugs lazy, and birds are just starting to sing again. It's a great time for camping and being outside. Some days you can open the windows; some, it's still too cold.

Sprunner

For Central Texas, this is the time that moist warmth begins to creep into everything. "Sprunner" begins in April but really gets going in May. Hopefully, spring rains have drenched us with exciting thunderstorms, and another wave of wildflowers begins, which consists of cactus flowers (my favorite), bee balm, and white prickly poppy along with blanket flowers and other wildflowers creating a chorus of color all over open fields—anywhere that is semiprotected from grazing becomes a visual symphony of violets, white, pink, red, orange, and yellow blooms.

Again this is all dependent on how much rain and how hot we get how quickly. I do think that as far as color goes, April is the prettiest time to be in Central Texas. Summer really begins when the humidity and temperatures soar and stay up there. In sprunner, the temperatures may teeter back and forth, but what marks summer as summer is when they stay.

June starts out as fun and you may still have pretty wildflowers blooming and lots of fun visiting local swimming holes. Everyone and everything wakes up. We become full of critters, creeping, crawling, flying, stinging, and biting. The further west you get, the less buggy. Birds get their fill of critters, and we get our fill of them too. Our gardens are usually established by now, many common garden herbs are ready for their first harvest and to be pruned back. Seasonal fruits include peaches, plums, mulberries, and loquats.

Summer

If it's a good year, and we have adequate water (which doesn't happen as much anymore), many spring plants can make it into July. Usually the rain peters out at this point and we watch things begin to dry up and bake, including us. Most people, critters, and plants find any way they can to avoid the heat. Swimming holes are full to bursting.

Some dominant summer plants include bull nettle (ouch), white sweet clover, mimosa blooms, slender vervain, and sages in bloom. Most plants are beginning to hunker down for the sun blizzard. Now is what I call time to slow down, either leave or move through the summer soup, and try to get through it.

Shade cloths are usually donned on gardens, and fruits are gathered. Shade beds with mints seem to do well in summer, even into the dog days. Native persimmons are ready.

Sumautumn

This late summer time can last all the way into October. "Sumautumn" persists from August until we get a break in the heat, usually from a tropical depression that comes up our way with some rain to cool us off. Temperatures can waver up and down. Anyone who has stayed through the summer is pretty brain-dead from the heat and sometimes depressed. Many garden plants will pant through August only to finally putter out when the heat finally wavers and they can relax. Then they die.

What plants make it through this heat? In Central Texas the plants most often noticed blooming at this time of year are wax mallow, trumpet creeper, and sunflowers, and even later, gumweed, goldenrod, and lobelia. Our gardens are pruned way back and covered with mulch to keep things alive. Prickly pear fruits ripen.

Autumn

Autumn comes with wetter, cooler weather, usually by mid-October into December. A fall bloom of sneezeweed and passionflower will kick in at this point. Pecans and walnuts begin to ripen and fall. Depending on the weather patterns, we may have flowers bloom into fall, and certainly you start seeing chile pequins on the bushes and juniper berries forming.

Our winter gardens are planted at the first sign of cooler weather, and we get ready to have drier, cooler times. Bugs begin to die. Critters slow down. We usually have several exciting thunderstorms and even a tornado or two. This is the best time to plant perennials. It allows time for their roots to become established and deep in preparation for the heat of next summer. It's a better time to plant biennials as well, including artichokes, fennel, dill, and mullein.

I always have better results planting in the fall. It is a wonderful time to get outside for Texans. Windows and doors stay open as much as possible to enjoy.

Winterish

The winterish months are a barren, brown time for wild plants but not for garden plants or invasive, useful winter weeds. Winter starts with a cold snap when suddenly we walk outside and realize shorts and flip-flops won't cut it. Jackets and socks and shoes are pulled out, and sometimes we try to find more than one glove. The amusing thing is that we may be 28°F for a day or two, then back up to 70°F and wearing shorts.

This is a great time to seed wildflowers. Winter gardens are full of cilantro, chickweed, cleavers, borage, and calendula mixed in with carrots, beets, lettuce, and broccoli. Roses bloom in late winter, along with dandelions, anemones, and henbit. Citrus trees begin to ripen. Depending on how far south you are, you may or may not freeze. No matter where you are in Texas, if a freeze is coming, everyone freaks out and shuts everything down and hunkers down as if a blizzard is upon us.

Winter is my favorite time for gardening. The cycle begins again. Such are the semiseasons of Texas.

WHY EAT WEEDS?
THE BENEFITS OF WILD FOODS

There are no words that truly capture the fulfillment and joy of living as a wild gardener. To pick one's way carefully into a sea of mouth-watering prickly pears, their spiny arms offering big, juicy red fruits as far as the eye can see, is an incredible experience. I collected over thirty pounds of prickly pear *tunas* last fall in Elgin, and I kept thinking over and over how lucky I was to have access to such a plentiful crop and how ridiculous it is not to take advantage of this native weed.

I love weeds. I plant them in my garden and help spread them—dandelion, chickweed, and more. Some of my favorite foods and medicines are very misunderstood, underused, and looked at with disdain when they pop up in a lawn or garden.

Wild foods are an essential part of my diet. I seek them out and try to add a leaf or flower to my meals whenever possible. Just as eating organic, whole, and living/raw foods tastes and feels better, so does consuming wild food. Wild foods help us to reconnect with our environment and offer resilience and balance. If I feel spacey or frustrated with the world, I oftentimes walk out to the fields surrounding my living space and find a leaf or berry to chew on. It helps bring me back to my center. Wild foods can be less glamorous or sexy than store-bought veggies but make up for it many times over in nutrition and the vital energy they possess. Stinging nettle leaves and chickweed are packed full of protein, iron, calcium, and many other nutrients. Teas or dishes made with these plants are exquisite additions to meals, and the nutrients are easier for our bodies to recognize and assimilate than most vitamin pills. These foods offer something that carefully planted and nurtured garden or farm-grown vegetables and fruits can't. The wild plant is free from human control and is forced to adapt to stresses which can make their nutrition and medicine more powerful. When a plant is spoiled with water, fertilizer, and pesticides, it doesn't have to work very hard and therefore alkaloids and other chemicals and nutrients can be less concentrated. This is similar for our bodies. When we pump them full of pharmaceuticals instead of letting them adapt and work out stresses themselves, we weaken our own immune systems.

Eating wild foods is a wonderful addition for anyone pursuing the raw foods lifestyle. As soon as plants are picked, they begin losing their constituents. The closer your connection from earth to mouth, the more you get out of your food.

Harvesting wild foods takes work and adds a deeper appreciation for what you take into your body. It is a lot harder to waste something you spent several hours collecting. Collecting can be made into an all-day adventure or be as simple as walking around your yard or a nearby park that doesn't get sprayed with pesticides. Either way it is always a pleasure. Harvesting your own food also adds presence of mind to the entire eating experience. A simple way to begin is to learn to properly identify the wild plants growing around your garden or lawn (don't use pesticides or pick things where your dog likes to sniff) and try snacking on a leaf or flower.

Whether it's yucca root, dewberries, morel mushrooms, pecans, or chickweed, I encourage you to investigate one or many of the countless wild foods surrounding Central Texas.

What is a Nutritive Herb?

These herbs owe their names to the nutritive values they provide to the diet. They are true foods and exert some mild medicinal effects. They provide the protein, carbohydrates, fats, vitamins, and minerals necessary for good nutrition. Sometimes they even improve assimilation of nutrients. These herbs can be eaten in meals as part of our daily dietary needs. Some may be dried and drunk as teas as a sort of "multivitamin."

Nutritional Benefits of Some Common Weeds

Alfalfa	*Medicago sativa*

Contains minerals such as calcium, magnesium, phosphorus, & potassium. High in chlorophyll, biotin, choline, inositol, iron, magnesium, PABA, phosphorus, potassium, protein, sodium, sulfur, tryptophan (an amino acid),& vitamins A, B-complex, C, D, E, K, P

Chickweed	*Stellaria media*

Contains significant amounts of calcium, iron, magnesium, phosphorous, potassium, zinc, manganese, beta-carotene, and niacin.

Dandelion	*Taraxacum officinale*

Contains significant amounts of protein, fiber, calcium, iron, magnesium, phosphorus, potassium, beta-carotene, vitamins C and E.

Lamb's Quarters	*Chenopodium berlandieri*

Good source of protein, fiber, calcium, iron, phosphorus, beta-carotene, and B vitamins.

Nettles	*Urtica spp*

High in protein, calcium, iron, magnesium, phosphorus, potassium, zinc, manganese, B vitamins, and vitamin C.

Oat Grass	*Avena sativa*

Contains silica, iron, calcium, copper, magnesium, manganese, zinc,& B vitamins.

Sow Thistle	*Sonchus oleraceus*

More vitamin A than spinach and a good quantity of vitamin C, calcium, phosphorus, iron, and a small amount of B vitamins.

Purslane	*Portulaca oleracea*

A good source of thiamin, niacin, vitamin B6 and folate, and a very good source of vitamin A, vitamin C, riboflavin, calcium, iron, magnesium, phosphorus, potassium, copper, and manganese.

A NOTE ON WILDCRAFTING

FORAGING AND THE PROPER HARVESTING AND COLLECTION OF WILD PLANT MATERIAL

This book is not a guide to teach you how to collect plants from the wild. I feel strongly that this type of knowledge is best learned from elder herbalists who have learned many tricks, tips, and what *not* to do over the years. It is also a lifestyle and lifelong path and commitment. As soon as you touch something in the wild, I believe you have made a personal commitment to that place to come back and steward the land. With that said I am going to include some thoughts on wildcrafting and doing so in Texas.

General Wildcrafting

Just what is wildcrafting? Wildcrafting is foraging plants from wild spaces. Many medicinal and cosmetic herbal products have labels on them saying wildcrafted or organic. This label is by no way a measure of how sustainably the plant was gathered. It is one step up from conventionally grown, but many companies know how to market things without providing a solid base to any claims. Wildcrafting is collecting plants from the wild. It has nothing to do with the person who is collecting having any ethical considerations towards how much or where. There are no guidelines wildcrafters are held to except their own. I spent many days calling up the mid- to large-sized herbal supply companies and inquiring as to what standards they required of wildcrafters. Only one or two of them had any standards at all, and one said "Well, they are wildcrafters, so we trust that they know what they are doing."

If you choose to be a wildcrafter or obtain plants from wildcrafters, then it is best to choose small companies owned by herbalists that have a direct connection to the land they harvest from or just herb lovers who are great foragers and know the land and respect it. If you choose to wildcraft then I strongly believe you must train with an experienced herbalist, one who has spent many years in the field and subscribes to the same ethics you do. As a great teacher of mine, Howie Brounstein, once said, "It's easy to pick, it's hard not to."

He also said "wildcrafting is stewardship" and if you always think in this manner, then you will soon see that over 95% of wildcrafting is not picking, it is being a keen observer and working with the land.

Even organically labeled plants can sometimes have been ripped from the wild and sold as organic after they have grown in organic farms for a few years.

I have chosen a new title for myself and my students: weedcrafter. Weedcrafting is harvesting plant material from the wild in a way that helps support the native ecosystem. I see weedcrafting as a type of wild gardening. A typical scenario would be to take a look at the native ecosystem you are working in, figure out ecologically what is out of balance, and harvest the medicinal plants that help bring the ecosystem back to balance. An example of this in Central Texas would be to harvest ligustrum or vitex, since both have escaped into the wildlands and can create issues with the local ecosystem. Gardeners also know that there are ways and times to collect that actually encourage growth and can help plants be more prolific. This is a better method for collecting some of the less common native plant material. If I do ever choose to harvest from the wild after careful study and observation, I then commit myself to that stand. From then on I make a vow that I will return to monitor and watch that stand. You would be surprised just how many herbalists are doing such things right now, even in the deepest, most remote parts of the world.

Why protect the wild and even worry at all about wildcrafting? Wildlands are being decimated at accelerated paces worldwide as our population grows. Just think, you may be in the middle of a place that gets sold to a development company and some large Mall-wart will cover up the last wild stand of echinacea in the area. This is happening daily. Just because we have large areas of weedy land or land that isn't being used, doesn't mean that it's in good shape and has a healthy level of diversity or that it's not going to be sold.

Why worry about native plants? It's about climax communities, folks. Our native bioregion developed over time to create a balanced and healthy ecosystem able to keep going year after year. These communities balance not only plant life, but animal and insect life as well. Humans have introduced wildcards, non-native plants, that have thrown this balance to the wind and created cycles ending in less diverse, less sustainable, and more unhealthy ecosystems. It is important to be conscious of our impact and leave wildlands alone as much as possible by cleaning up, taking photos rather than picking, packing in and packing out. The less disturbance the better. A good wildcrafter is always collecting and spreading native seeds . If you are in a gorgeous wild stand of plants ripe with fruit falling on the ground or seeds ready to drop, then you can go ahead and take no more than 10% of 10% of each plant's seeds. That means you need to count seeds!

Why do people wildcraft? Many plants can be grown, and this is always a primary choice for creating a first aid kit for you and your family. Some herbal practitioners believe that the vitality and strength of plant material gathered from the wild is more potent or is of a higher quality than plants that are garden grown and fussed over with watering, fertilizer, and mulch. Wild plants have to work hard to survive and so it is believed that if anything, the energetics of the plant could be more powerful or the constituents more concentrated. Wildcrafting can be a good choice for those that have land and are learning to steward it. For those who live in cities, growing is probably a better choice, unless you have created close alliances with one or more land owners. Most people do not need to wildcraft, and though it is quite thrilling to find a rare and powerful medicinal plant in the wild, it is best to take pictures and act as its steward. Many folks who are learning to wildcraft end up collecting things they do not really need or way too much. Before you ever pick a plant, your first question should always be: Do I really *need* this plant? What am I going to use it for? Then go through a checklist like the one found below.

Many herbalists have created rating systems to define the safest to most endangered plants for wildharvesting. The ratings I teach to students categorize plants in six levels of impact on the ecosystem. The safest plants to harvest are those in danger of otherwise being lost and those that are very prolific. Rare and threatened species should almost never be taken from the wild.

Levels of Impact on Wild Stands

Think bioregionally! When choosing what to harvest and what not to, you can use the guidelines shown below. Level 1 plants have the least amount of impact and Level 6 plants have the most amount of impact.

1	Rescues	Plant material that needs to be rescued from destruction or has been blown off by a storm or some other unseen force. For example, a fallen cottonwood branch or a field of yarrow about to be bulldozed for an apartment complex.
2	Weedy non-natives	Plants that have been brought in from other places and now spread invasively in Central Texas, such as mullein and vitex.
3	Weedy natives and non-weedy non-natives	Local plants that grow pervasively like cactus, and foreign species that grow in the local ecosystem, such as lemon balm.
4	Non-weedy natives	Plants that grow in balance should be harvested with care. Plants like agarita and prickly ash can be lightly pruned with minimal risk to the plant population.
5	Native, less common, and plants at risk from overharvesting or habitat destruction	These plants should be rarely harvested, if at all, and only after years of careful observation of an area. Lobelia is an example of a threatened species.
6	Endemic plants, plants that can't be propagated, federally endangered species, & rare/ sensitive native plants	Do not pick. Seed and propagate in home or wild gardens if possible. For example, the *Mahonia swaseyi* species of agarita, wild orchids, and our native echinaceas are all no picks.

Wildcrafting and Weedcrafting in Texas

Talk about challenging—wildcrafting in a place with no public lands! That means that I have made a lot of land owner alliances over the years. In exchange for providing knowledge of what useful plants grew on their land, I received a place to harvest. As my focus shifted more to weedcrafting, it became even easier. I go into areas and harvest so that it makes the ecosystem stronger, and I collect plants that are common. Wildcrafting in Texas means: Be ready to sweat, be pricked, bitten, stung, burnt, and be patient. We have some amazing medicinal plants here. Growing your favorites will really help you be able to find them in the wild and become a great steward to them.

Being a wild gardener and weedcrafter means:

- ∞ *Creating small community gardens all over the cities is essential. They can function as seed banks for wild plants that are being decimated from habitat loss.*

- ∞ *Always collect seeds from unusual plants, spread them, and try to grow them.*

- ∞ *Rescue plant material from areas that are being developed, even taking the entire plant if possible.*

- ∞ *Offer information to land owners as to what plants are worth propagating, especially if they are native or endemic to the region.*

- ∞ *Take notes, steward the land and leave offerings if you take from an area. Cornmeal, tobacco, water, songs, and even pee are great offerings.*

23

WILDSCAPING AND WILDSEEDING

Wildscapes are typically defined as semimanaged areas on one's property where a majority of native plants and some other well-adapted species are grown to attract and benefit wildlife by offering food, water, and shelter. These areas can also be a source of medicinal plants useful for many home first aid situations and as food for humans. Wildscaping is a way each of us can help offset habitat destruction and increase biodiversity in our communities. Wildseeding is a similar concept in which plants are integrated into wild habitat by broadcasting seeds of native plants. Wildseeding of plants can be done in a similar fashion to wildscaping and may be a viable source of income in rural areas. In this chapter I am highlighting a selection of native medicinal and edible plants that can be wildscaped, wildseeded, or wildgrown. Edible and medicinal wildscapes create direct connections between the health of our native ecosystems and the health of humans. There is a belief in many holistic medical systems that using seasonal plants adapted to your environment is a better choice when bringing your body into balance and health.

Harvesting of Plant Material

The way plant material is harvested for human use can actually benefit the wildscape or wildseeded land. Harvesting plant material can be incorrectly assumed to create habitat destruction or injure plants. On the other end of the spectrum, it is sometimes assumed that just because one harvests plant material, they have an understanding of how to do so in a sustainable way. Both assumptions arencorrect. It is essential that people foraging plant material, especially from the wild, be well-trained. Botanical identification is important, but being able to evaluate the best and most conservative way to take plant material may also be of benefit to the stand of plants in question. I call this approach to harvesting a form of wild gardening—eco-herbalism or eco-foraging. Considerations to keep in mind when harvesting include the part of plant harvested, time of year plant material is harvested, soil type, rainfall, and whether the stand of plants needs some sort of tending (grass pulled, branches thinned, composting). Strategies for ensuring plants are benefitted by human interference involve harvesting when plant is going to seed, spreading and collecting seeds, looking for alternatives to harvesting roots (tubers or side-shoot rhizomes usually work, sometimes aboveground parts can be used instead). If it is a drought year, maybe hold back on consuming food or medicine unless it is an emergency so that wildlife gets first dibs. If bark is needed, never debark a tree; prune smaller limbs and debark those. By employing thoughtful harvesting strategies, you ensure that everyone, including the plants, is well tended.

Table 1 represents a brief selection of native plants that grow well in wildscapes and also offer medicinal or edible benefits. The selection of native plants are not only chosen for their ethnobotanical evidence, folk usage and modern use, but as plants I have personally collected and used in my practice as an herbalist in Central Texas. I, my students, and my clients, have eaten and/or experienced these plants effectiveness as first aid and food. Many times the difference between medicine and poison may be by the part used, whether the plant needs some sort of preparation to make it safe for use, dosage, or making sure you have the correct species. With our native species, we have many variables and some species may be more or less potent than what is in the popular market now. Also to consider is that the person's own vital response may be different because their biochemistry is slightly altered than someone else's. Herbalism can be frustrating to many scientists because there are so many gray areas. All of these things take training and experience to differentiate. *Just because something is edible doesn't mean it is palatable.* I have chosen some plants that taste good and have medicinal value. This table represents a glimpse at a few of the herbs I teach about and use as an herbal medicine educator and herbal practitioner in Central Texas.

The following table of native Texas edible and medicinal plants is a glimpse at some suggestions for home owners, plant nursery owners, farmers, and land owners to encourage propagation or grow for market. I hope to redefine some plants seen as weeds into useful and exciting plants to care for. The column under Wild Crop indicates whether or not the plant can be developed as a wild crop. These plants attract important pollinators that are part of our native ecosystems. Butterflies, bumblebees, native birds and small mammals all benefit from the wild flora. My small, city yard has become host to not only many kinds of useful native edible and medicinal plants, but in the short time I have been there, more and more critters have found their way into my gardens. Turtles, toads, garden snakes, butterflies, moths, dragonflies and many native birds all share the yard with my family. Every year I build new beds and increase my medicine cabinet and native food sources as well as sharing the bounty with the surrounding critters.

Edible, Medicinal, & Wildlife Uses	Description & Growing Considerations	Harvesting & Preparation	Wild Crop
AGARITA	*Mahonia trifoliolata* (formerly *Berberis trifoliolata*)		
Antimicrobial bitter, contains berberine, used to treat digestive and other infections. Berries eaten in jellies, and wines. Attracts bees, insects. birds. and small mammals	Large, prickly perennial shrub found in full sun to part shade. I have found it all over Central Texas, seeming to prefer rocky Hill Country and Blackland gumbo soils. Likes to grow under larger trees, such as Juniper. Wildseeding as an understory may have more success. Some species seem susceptible to fungal infections.	Aboveground parts harvested in spring. Berries in late spring/early summer. Roots are not necessary for potent extract, branches are preferred. Made into powder, tea, tincture, or oil.	Yes Need more research here
BEE BALM			*Monarda spp*
All parts of the plant have high levels of thymol, an anti-infective. Used for fungal and other infections. Culinary spice. Attracts bees and wasps. (1)	Full-sun, showy, annual to perennial, mint-family wildflower with whorls of flowers up stem, 1-2 feet tall. Flowers vary in color from pink to white depending on species. Extremely aromatic. I have found in Central Texas and East Texas prairies and open fields in late spring and early summer.	Entire plant can be harvested in summer when going into seed. Made into tincture, oil, honey, tea, or spritzer.	Yes
BUTTERFLY WEED*			*Asclepias tuberosa*
Assists in resolving phlegm in lung infections, roots prepared and eaten by the Sioux, in some species the pods are prepared and eaten. (2) Nectar source and larval host. Same color as the monarch butterflies it attracts.	Perennial wildflower with brilliant orange flowers. Sun to part shade. In Central Texas, I have found it growing just east of Austin, mainly in the Lost Pines. Seems to grow best in slightly acidic, well-drained, sandy or gravelly soil. Have found it is hard to keep alive in first year. Watch for adulteration in nursery market where non-natives are being sold.	Root is harvested at maturity in fall. Usually processed into tea or tincture. (3)	Yes Need more research here

CARDINAL FLOWER — *Lobelia cardinalis*

Strong drop-dosage antispasmodic used internally and externally to relieve painful muscular spasming. Attracts ruby throated hummingbirds. (1)	Tall perennial wildflower found in the Hill Country with spectacular red blooms. Grows best in part sun to shade and likes wet feet. Found in the wild mostly in waterways or on the sides of waterways. Could do well as a pond plant.	Harvest aboveground parts while in flower and going to seed. Made into fresh tincture, vinegar, or oil.	Yes, in or near water Needs research

GUMWEED — *Grindelia spp*

Aromatic and resinous, expectorant. Tends to soothe spasms and dry up secretions, used to treat poison ivy.	Full to part sun wildflower with yellow blooms in the hottest and driest times of year. Notable shiny look to leaves and stems. I have seen growing in the Hill Country.	Harvest aboveground parts while in flower and going into seed, usually late summer	Maybe

PASSIONFLOWER — *Passiflora spp*

Antianxiety agent and sedative, relaxes heart and promotes more restful sleep. Fruits are eaten.	Perennial vine found in full sun to shade with unusual flowers that can bloom more than one time per year. Some species make large edible fruits in late spring/early summer. Tough and drought tolerant.	Harvest leaves and flowers into tea, tincture, or glycerite. Fruits can be in summer to early fall.	Yes

PURPLE CONEFLOWER* — *Echinacea spp*

Immune stimulant used to draw poison out of the body, topically and internally. Relieves pain from venomous bites and stings. Attracts bumblebees and insects.	Showy pink perennial wildflower. All species grow well in Central Texas. Have found a solitary native in the Lost Pines and a lone native stand* east towards Giddings. Grows well in full sun. May need some irrigation if growing for market.	Root (at least 3 years old) and seeds harvested in fall. Made into tea, tincture, glycerite, paste, or powder. Pups may be pulled from main root and replanted.	Yes, but may need irrigation for high yields

PRICKLY ASH — *Zanthoxylum spp*

Circulatory stimulant, warming, analgesic and antimicrobial, popular folk remedy for toothaches. Used in Chinese and Western herbal medicine.	Full- to part-sun tree, species varying in height. Citrus family plant with shiny pinnate leaves and spines all over. Some species make large clusters of dark bluish berries.	Woody parts, leaves, and berries collected in spring. Made into tincture or tea.	Yes

PRICKLY PEAR CACTUS			*Opuntia spp*
Stabilizes blood sugar and soothes to mucous membranes. Helps with burns, diarrhea, and ulcers. Pads, *tunas*, and flowers all used as food and first aid.	Full-sun. large shrub, very weedy. Will spread easily, some would say too easily. Has prominent display of flowers, most common species in Central Texas has showy yellow blooms in spring, fruits in late summer to fall. Beware of spines.	Harvest pads all year round, flowers in spring, fruit in fall. Pads can be eaten, juiced, applied as a poultice; flowers as tea, tincture, or glycerite; *tunas* juiced into wine. (4)	No need, very weedy
VERVAIN			*Glandularia bipinnatifida* (formerly *Verbena bipinnatifida*) et al
Calming antianxiety remedy and diaphoretic. Relieves digestive stress and IBS-type conditions. Also used for cold and flu.	Full- to part-sun, perennial wildflower with purple to pink flowers. Other *Verbena* species vary in appearance.	Aboveground parts harvested while in flower or going to seed. Made into tea, tincture, or glycerite.	Maybe

• *Means at risk plant—may be subject to overharvesting in the wild according to United Plant Savers*

MATERIA MEDICA OF TEXAS

Common Name(s) ⚠ *Scientific name(s)*	Plant Family
Status – Tells if the plant is native, non-native, weedy, rare, or otherwise, and outlines the range of growth in Texas	[picture] See accompanying photobook for bigger and more detailed photos
🌿 Parts Used – Parts of plant generally used in making medicinal extracts	
▼ Time of Year – Best time of year to harvest the plant	
⚕ Actions – Medicinal actions the plant may have on the body	
⚗ Medicinal Preparation – Preferred type of preparation *Explanation* following this key	*Type of Plant – A general description of the plant's characteristics*
Other Uses – Any other uses noted	
Herbal First Aid – Ways you may be able to use this plant for first aid	
Special Notes – Includes toxicities or lookalikes to note, folklore, and personal experience with the plant	

Key to Materia Medica Charts

⚠ This symbol indicates potential toxicities or important cautions for handling the plant. Look for details in the special notes section.

📖 Expanded monographs are available on a select number of the following plants as a workbook entitled *Medicinal Plant Allies of the Wildflower School*, used in the Wildflower Community Herbalism Program, available off our website given in the resources section of the book

Explanation of Preparations

The preferred medicinal preparation explains how to best extract the active compounds from the plant. This preference is personal, the ratio and percentage is based off of my experience as a herbalist. This section provides the type of solvent that may be used, such as alcohol, and the percentage of the solvent needed to get the most potent extract. The given ratios show the optimal proportion of solvent to plant.   For example, 1:5 means one part of solvent by volume to 5 parts of plant by weight. 96% would mean using grain alcohol.

Each Extract(Tincture, Vinegar, Glycerite, Infusion, Decoction) can be found further defined in the glossary at the end of the book. Where needed, fresh or dry indicate the best state for the plant at the start of the extraction process.

Native to region, more common from the Southerly Gulf coast, Rio Grande Valley increasing as one heads into West Texas. Prolific in Central Texas, can be weedy.

 Entire plant useful: root, stems, leaves, berries

 Flowers in late winter, berries in late spring

 Alterative, anti-microbial, bitter, stimulant

 Strong decoction of woody parts; or tincture woody parts 40% 1:2 fresh; leaves infuse in oil 1:5

Perennial evergreen shrub with bluish-green spiny, trifoliate leaflets, yellow flowers, and red berries

Dye (roots and branches), food source (berries)

Important bioregional first aid for both topical infections and internal infections related to the gastrointestinal tract, from mouth and gum infections to diarrhea. Stimulating to digestion and particularly important for use as a liver stimulant.

May be used as a replacement for other berberine-containing plants like *Berberis*, *Mahonia*, *Coptis*, or *Hydrastis* species. May be misidentified as a holly. Endemic and rarely found *Mahonia swaseyi* species is a no-touch. There is no need to collect the root as all woody parts are effective. Formerly named *Berberis trifoliolata*. I use this plant regularly in practice. Expanded monograph available.

Some species native to region, some are native to other deserts of the southwestern United States and northern Mexico. Horticultural varieties are used in xeriscaping all over Texas. Can be opportunistic and invasive due to rhizomatous growth.

 Entire plant is useful, root is medicinal

 Harvestable throughout year

 Anti-inflammatory, purgative, laxative, antimicrobial, anticancer

Perennial succulent with basal rosette of thick, pointed leaves ending in spines. Some species get quite large, up to 6 feet tall and wide. Produces a large showy cluster of white flowers on a tall stalk, fruits and then dies. Also spreads by rhizome.

 I have not used as a medicinal extract due to potential of contact dermatitis.

Food, fodder, paper, twine, soap, roofing, fencing, dye, soap, sweetener, and alcoholic drinks

Has a history of use to treat inflammatory conditions in the joints and around teeth and to relieve pain. (1) Has also been used topically on wounds as a binding agent and to kill infection. (2)

POTENTIAL TOXICITY: *Fresh sap of plant has produced contact dermatitis in some people.* I have not used this plant regularly in practice. May be confused with yucca. Agave syrup has been marketed as a natural sweetener, but studies show it raises blood sugar as much or more than corn syrup.

Amaranth, Pig Weed *Amaranthus spp* Amaranthaceae

Native, weedy, invasive, and opportunistic in disturbed areas all over Texas

 Leaves and seeds

 Easiest to notice when in seed, prolific in late summer through fall

 Nutritive, astringent, antioxidant

 None noted

Dye; Food source—leaves edible as potherb, young greens of some species as salad greens, seeds are edible

Annual to perennial (depending on species) herb, alternating simple leaves, with the top of the plant terminating in large, sometimes even drooping seed heads mainly in fall. Can get quite tall, 3-5 feet.

Useful astringent, that soothes inflammation, cuts, scrapes, and burns topically. Some sources cite this as being a useful styptic, that stops bleeding. (3)

CAUTION: *Use young shoots of leaves due to potential toxicities with older leaves.* Chickens love the seed heads. Tasty cooked green. I use this plant occasionally in practice and more often as an food.

American Beautyberry	*Callicarpa americana*	Verbenaceae

Native to region; found more commonly Central to North and East Texas. Prefers swamps, moist woodlands, and coastal areas.	
Leaves and berries	
Late summer to fall	
Aromatic, antimicrobial, diaphoretic, stomachic	*Perennial deciduous shrub with large clusters of purple berries that stay attached after the leaves drop in the fall.*
None noted	
Edible berries can be made into jams, jellies, wine, and more	

Several tribes used/use beautyberry to treat things like colic, dysentery, and fevers. The aromatic leaves have been used as a deterrent for both flies and mosquitos. The plant's aromatic properties are currently being researched as an insect repellent. Parts of the plant are also being investigated as a cancer-fighting remedy (4).

Originally, berries were rumored to be toxic, but experiences by many locals eating it regularly leads one to question this assumption. I use this plant occasionally in practice and most often, the leaves as an insect repellent.

American Groundnut	*Apios americana*	Fabaceae

Native; quite common in East Texas, preferring moister soils in forests	
Tubers	
None noted	
Folk use suggests astringent, anti-inflammatory, and vulnerary actions	*Vining perennial with pinnately compound leaves and showy pinkish flowers.*
None noted	
Edible tubers are so tasty they are being investigated for commercial viability	

Few ethnobotanical references suggest any type of medicinal use, those that do cite using tubers mashed and applied to treat proud flesh, a condition in which there is overgranulation of flesh over a wound (5). The presence of allantoin suggests that it not only relieves overproduction but also helps in healing process. Used in vet care, especially with horses.

Most of the information related to groundnut relates to its use as a wild food being not just edible but also tasty!

Bee Balm, Horsemint, Wild Oregano	*Monarda citriodora, M. punctata, et. al.*	Lamiaceae

Native and prolific, found in open fields in full sun throughout Texas

 Whole plant, including root

 Late spring to early summer

 Aromatic, stimulant, disinfectant, antiviral, antifungal

Infused honey; tincture 96% 1:2 fresh; infused oil 1:5 dry

Dye—yellow; Food source—greens can be eaten before flowering, or else they get bitter

Annual wildflower with showy terminal whorls of flowers ranging from pink to purple to yellow depending on the species. Leaves are linear and the plant grows to about a foot to a foot and a half tall.

Aboveground parts are an important disinfectant and antimicrobial. This is Wild Oregano, and may be used similarly to Oregano medicinally.. The herb has an affinity to the throat. It is also helpful in the treatment of candidiasis and fungal infections in the lungs. Repels insects.

I use this plant regularly in practice. Expanded monograph available.

Black-Eyed Susan | *Rudbeckia hirta* | Asteraceae

Native, but sparse. Mostly found in open prairies in Southeast Texas.

 Root for medicine, leaves and flowers for dye

 Fall

 Immunostimulant (6)

 Decoction; tincture 96% 1:2

Dye—yellow; food source— greens can be eaten before flowering, or else they get bitter (7)

Mainly annual wildflower with bright yellow, composite flower head. The dark center arrangement protrudes upwards with the ray flowers drooping down around it.

Can be used like Echinacea to help stimulate the body to respond against infection. Can use topically to draw out poisons and to alleviate pain.

I have not used this plant regularly in practice. Easy to propagate in the garden.

38

| Blackhaw | *Viburnum rufidulum, V. dentatum* | Caprifoliaceae |

Native, more common the farther north and east you go in Texas. I usually find it along waterways in Central Texas but also scattered throughout East Texas.

 Woody parts

 Spring

 Antispasmodic, sedative

 Tincture 96% 1:2, fresh, using leaves, small twigs and stems

Perennial deciduous tree with white clusters of blooms in early spring, turning to blue-black berries, simple, shiny opposite leaves

The berries of *V. rufidulum* and some other species have a history of being eaten as jams and jellies (8).

Used to treat abdominal cramping, especially menstrual cramps, and to soothe generalized muscular soreness and pain.

Can look like a dogwood initially, but has defining characteristics and blooms earlier. I use this plant regularly in practice.

Boneset   *Eupatorium perfoliatum, et al*   Asteraceae

Native, more common in East and North Texas		
	Aboveground, in flower	
	Spring	
	Diaphoretic, antiviral, febrifuge, laxative, immunostimulant, antitumor	*Perennial herb topped with dense clusters of white flowers and simple linear leaves that spiral down, clasping around the stem. Grows 2-4 feet tall.*
	Hot infusion; tincture 96% 1:2, fresh	
No other uses noted.		

Popular historical remedy used against influenza (9). Helps to break a fever and recover from a cold by producing a sweat (10). Has a history of use in helping with deep aches in the bones accompanied by fever. Has been found to be effective against herpes (11).

I recently started to harvest the local species it in the wild and am beginning to use it in practice. No notes as of yet.

Brahmi, Herb of Grace	*Bacopa monnieri*	Scrophulariaceae

Native, commonly found in marshy waterways		
Whole plant		
Fall		
Antioxidant, alterative, trophorestorative to nervous system, sedative	*Perennial wetland herb, creeping and sprawling into waterways with tiny, simple succulent leaves and 5-petaled white flowers*
None noted. Traditionally used as a tea or tincture.	
B. caroliniana is noted as edible, with a lime scent and flavor. Both *B. caroliniana* and *B. monnieri* are high in vitamin C.	

Popular in Ayurvedic medicine; being used to help improve memory in the elderly (12) and as a diuretic and energizer for the heart and respiratory system (13). Seems to create a normalizing and/or sedative effect on the nervous system. Has been used to treat the effects of Alzheimers (14).

I do not use this plant regularly in practice except as a massage oil, specifically when doing head and neck work or Ayurvedic treatments.

Brickelbush, Prodigiosa	*Brickellia laciniata, B. cylindracea, B. eupatorioides, et al*	Asteraceae

Native, many species extend from west Texas through northeast Texas		
Leaves		
Spring		
Bitter, spasmolytic, hypoglycemic action, gastroprotective (15)		*Annual to perennial wildflower or shrub depending on species, with yellow discoid inflorescences and sticky, sandpapery linear leaves.*
Hot tea, used regularly		
No other uses noted.		

Some species of this genus are used to help stabilize blood sugar levels in diabetics. May also be useful in treating cataracts (16). Relieves stomachaches and gas pain.

Herbalist Michael Moore, was adamant that this plant's effectiveness had to be delivered in a tea. I do not use this plant regularly in practice.

Bull Nettle	 *Cnidoscolus texanus*	Euphorbiaceae

Native; Central to East Texas	
Nutlets, root	
Spring to summer	
Antiviral	*Perennial wildflower with milky latex and glowing white flowers, leaves are simple and alternate with 3-5 lobes, the most distinguishing characteristic being the glistening, stinging hairs that cover the plant.*
None	
Food source—nutlets	

No known herbal first aid uses. The juice of the root is said to cure the sting of the plant. Recently, some antiviral compounds have been identified in the plant. (17)

Another species, known as Chaya, is used as a nutritive "super nettle" potherb in Mexico; this species may be too toxic. I do not use this plant regularly in practice, but I have made a flower essence and eaten the nutlets.

Native, found distributed wild throughout Texas, often near water

 Twigs

 Summer to fall

 Astringent, bitter, tonic, aromatic, laxative, cholagogue

Decoction; tincture 96% 1:2, fresh

Attracts butterflies!

Perennial shrub with white, showy, fragrant, spherical inflorescences with protruding stamens

Aids in sluggish digestion, gastrointestinal congestion, stimulates bile secretion, laxative, tonic (18) cholagogue

There are some potentially toxic glycosides in the plant (19). Best for short-term use. I do not use this plant regularly in practice.

Non-native; garden plant (easily grown throughout winter, with little protection depending on how deep it freezes). Easily started by direct seed in fall.

 Aboveground parts may be used while flowering

 Winter to early spring

 Immunomodulatory, antimicrobial, vulnerary

 Tincture 50% 1:2; dried flowers macerated 1:5 in oil

Dye—has been used as a replacement to saffron as a yellow dye for cheese, Food source— flowers are edible (20)

Annual non-native garden flower with yellow to orange flowers and delicate, light green, simple, sticky, elliptical leaves with tiny hairs covering them. Grows as a singular clump with a few blooms not over 8-12 inches until spring. After this point its blooms may start to get smaller and longer.

Used topically to help resolve skin infections and wounds; also used internally. Tends to promote healing of mucosal tissues.

I use this plant regularly in practice. Expanded monograph available.

Native, weedy; Central and South Texas

 Aboveground

 Fall

 Aromatic, analgesic , antifungal, anti-inflammatory , antioxidant (21; 22)

Tincture 96% 1:2, fresh; oil 1:5, dry

Annual to perennial semi-evergreen wildflower with yellow flowers, simple, grayish green hairy alternate leaves. Plant is aromatic.

No other uses known.

Used to treat arthritic conditions and fungal infections; acute pain from injury to tissues (19).

Common adulterant in arnica products sold on the market (does not have the same constituents or indications). Herbalist Charles Kane differentiates arnica from camphorweed, saying use true arnica for subacute injuries to bring in the immune-stimulating response; use camphorweed to help alleviate pain from tissue damage. This plant is newer to my practice.

Candelilla	*Euphorbia antisyphilitica*	Euphorbiaceae
Native to West Texas		
Modified stems		
Not known		
Purgative, analgesic		*Perennial, succulent, shrubby plant forming clumps of long, linear, tubular, grayish-green stems all reaching upwards, covered with a waxy coating tipped with a reddish fruit*
None known		
Wax is obtained from the modified stems.		

Used in Mexico to treat headaches and toothaches, was thought to be effective against syphilis, which gave the plant its scientific name (23).

Wax used in body care and cosmetics as a native alternative to beeswax. Take care to find out about how the wax is obtained as commercial use has led to unsustainable harvesting practices. I have used the wax, which requires a higher melting point and is slightly harder than beeswax.

Cardinal Flower, Lobelia	*Lobelia cardinalis*	Campanulaceae

Native, but not very common throughout Texas except in and around waterways. They really like wet feet. Found more towards far East and far West Texas

 Aboveground only

 Fall

 Calming, antispasmodic, emetic, gastric stimulant, diffusive

 Vinegar and/or Tincture 96% 1:2, fresh

Exceptionally beautiful, perennial wildflower growing up to 8 feet tall and terminating in arrangements of bright red flowers

No other uses noted.

Plants of this genus have a long history of use as powerful and complex medicinals. Popular folk use includes the relief of spasms and pain in the respiratory tract(asthmatic) and muscles. It may also help to curb nicotine cravings (24).

CAUTION: *Use in drop dosages under the guidance of an experienced practitioner. Too much can make you nauseous.* Must use fresh plant to gain benefits from all of its complex alkaloids; it loses several when dry. I do not use this in practice because I have never seen enough to harvest. Sporadic at best in Central Texas.

Carolina Jessamine	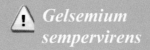 *Gelsemium sempervirens*	Apocynaceae

Non-native landscaping shrub

 Root

 Fall

Calming, cardiac sedative, analgesic, antispasmodic, febrifuge, diaphoretic	*Large, perennial evergreen shrub with long stems of leaves reaching up and away from the center. At varying times of the year it becomes covered with yellow flowers.*
Tincture 65% 1:2	
No other uses known.	

Strong central nervous system depressant activity, used to stop spastic asthma attacks, convulsions, neuralgia, and more. (25)

TOXIC: *Dangerous in high doses but effective in drop dosage.* Became known as the "Eclectic Febrifuge" due to a mistaken identification and a man taking a large dose of the plant and "discovering" it as a remedy (26) (27)

Cat's Claw Acacia, Huisache

Acacia greggii, A. farnesiana

Fabaceae

Native; abundant to Central, West, and South Texas, especially in limestone

 Stems, small branches, leaves and pods (powdered)

 Spring

 Anti-inflammatory, astringent, demulcent, antimicrobial, entheogenic

Gum in a tincture 96% 1:2, burned as incense

The perfume industry derives a scent from *A. farnesiana* referred to as *cassie*. (28)

Perennial shrubby tree, branches covered with thorns, leaves are pinnately compound with spherical to oblong discoid flowers yellow to white in color.

Soothing to inflamed skin. Woody parts taken internally help to stop diarrhea, soothe and calm coughs during respiratory infections.

Herbalist Michael Moore recommended this as a substitute for the well-known gum arabic.

Chaparral, Creosote Bush	*Larrea tridentata*	Zygophyllaceae

Native and weedy; all over West Texas		
	Leaves while in flower	
	After a rain, while in flower	
	Aromatic, bitter, astringent, antioxidant, vulnerary, antimicrobial	*Perennial shrubby tree with opposite resinous leaves and yellow shiny 5 petaled flowers turning into a little furry capsule. Very unique aromatics.*
	Decoction, oil 1:5, powder, tincture 96% 1:2	
Researched as a bioremediator to clean up heavy metals in the soil. (29)		

Used to shrink tumors, reduce pain of burns and other skin inflammation. Heals infections topically and internally. Extremely potent.

If planted in a garden, chaparral tends to inhibit the growth of other plants because it is so efficient at absorbing water. (30) The plant is ancient. There is a colony in the Mojave desert known as King Clone that is 11,700 years old. (31)

Chaparro Amargosa, Castela, Crucifixion Thorn	*Castela texana*	Simaroubaceae

Native; may be found in South and West Texas

 Modified stems

 Please don't pick unless emergency.

Vermifuge, antiamoebic (32)	*Shrubby, succulent, perennial tree made up of stems terminating in spines, tiny leaves, and orange flowers turning to small red round fruits.* C. emoryi *is pictured above*
Tincture or strong decoction	
No other uses known.	

Previously used as bitter parasite remedy, but now the desert variety is too fragile of a plant population. There is no data on use of the native variety in Texas.

DO NOT PICK. Wild populations have been decimated from improper harvest in the Desert Southwest. Need to learn how to wildcraft this properly from an actual herbalist before picking, or risk killing the entire tree (based on my personal experience).

Chasteberry, Vitex, Monk's Pepper	*Vitex agnus-castus*	Verbenaceae

Non-native, weedy, invasive; planted throughout Texas as fast growing drought tolerant shade trees. Biologists are now trying to mediate their escape into wildlands, which is disrupting native ecosystems.

 Berries

 Time of Year

 Early fall (when berries ripen and are easily stripped off of the limbs)

 Tincture 75% 1:2, fresh berries

Used as a spice. In ancient Rome, Vitex was carried by vestal virgins as a symbol of chastity and used at festivals like Thesmophoria to show chasteness, hence the name.

Perennial, deciduous, shrubby tree with purple flowers, turning to dense clusters of small dark berries in summer as they ripen. Leaves are palmately compound and grayish green. Plant has a bright, piercing, almost piney and sweet aroma.

Regulates reproductive hormones and take the edge off of addictive tendencies. Its most popular use is in helping to relieve hot flashes and regulate menses cycles. One of Austin herbalist, Ellen Zimmermann's favorites!

Have personally seen that this plant has now escaped into preserves and other wild areas of Central Texas; now listed as invasive. Expanded monograph available.

Non-native, invasive weed found in disturbed soils throughout Texas

 Aboveground leaves

 Most prolific in late summer and fall

 Demulcent, antimicrobial properties recently have been found in the plant

 Cold infusion

Annual herb with 5-petaled, small, pale, pinkish flowers, and simple roundish and lobed crinkly leaves with palmate venation. Grows to about 6 inches tall.

Food source (seed high in protein), but you need to be careful where you obtain the plant from as it has been shown to accumulate nitrates in the leaves. (33)

Soothes inflamed mucous membranes in throat, lungs, stomach, and urinary tract.

I do not recommend planting this, it is invasive and may be foraged easily. (34)

Chickweed	*Stellaria media*	Caryophyllaceae

Non-native, weedy; found in wetter areas of central, east, and north Texas, especially around lawns.

 Aboveground

 Winter to spring

 Emollient, anti-inflammatory, nutritive, vulnerary

 Tasty on salads, as a fresh juice, and pesto; fresh oil, wilted to 30% of weight 1:3; fresh plant vinegar, Simpler's method

Food source. Also great spring green for chickens, will help harden the shells of their eggs.

Annual herbaceous groundcover. Clumping herb with tender, delicate, reddish stems covered in tiny white flowers that look like 10 petals but are actually 5 deeply clefted petals.

Full of micronutrients, great as a "superfood,". Topically, soothing to skin conditions.

This is a favorite winter food and weed for me. I love to collect and shake seeds all over the garden to ensure more for next year. I highly recommend getting to know this plant! Expanded monograph available.

Native; especially prolific in Central to South Texas. Seems to prefer to grow along fences.

 Berries

 Fall to winter

 Styptic and aromatic, antimicrobial, rubefacient, analgesic, stimulant

 Tincture 96% 1:10; dried berries in oil 1:10

Culinary spice

Perennial shrub bearing small white flowers and tiny, bright red fruits when ripe. May be evergreen further south. Dies back to root in Central Texas. Grows from 2 feet to 4 feet tall and in diameter.

Can be used sparingly internally to help move circulation to the extremities; topically it helps to relieve pain and warm up cold, arthritic and muscular aches and pain.

CAUTION: *After touching berries, wash hands or prepare for a burn.* This must be used sparingly or tested since berries can vary in potency.

| Chinaberry | ⚠️ *Melia azedarach* | Meliaceae |

Non-native, weedy and very invasive; mostly Northeast, Central, and South Texas

 Leaves and berries

 Fall for berries

 Antimicrobial, antifungal, insecticidal

 Macerated berries in infusion

No other uses known.

Perennial tree with fragrant, pale-pink flowers forming white to yellow berries. The leaves are pinnately compound, and the tree is fast growing and shallowly rooted, often found rotting and breaking apart with new shoots emerging quickly.

May be used sparingly in sprays to repel and kill insects, fleas, aphids, and pests in general.

Do not ingest. May be more toxic than its cousin neem, though it shares some of the same properties. (35)

57

Cleavers, Stickyweed, Bedstraw — *Galium aparine, et al* — Rubiaceae

Non-native, weedy; central to east and north Texas, needs shady wet areas to get established. There is also a more uncommon native species that is a no pick because the non-native is so much more widely available.

	Aboveground vining parts while in flower, before going to seed
	Winter to spring
	Diuretic, lymphatic, urinary astringent
	Fresh juice, freeze into ice cubes; fresh glycerite 1:2 100%

Annual herbaceous vine with sticky hairs all over and leaves at intervals, forming whorls. Creates tiny white flowers.

Used like rennet to curdle cheese and some more aromatic species were used to stuff mattresses. Seeds may be roasted and used as a coffee substitute. (36)

Used to cool down inflammation and burns externally, internally to help move infection out of the body and soothe urinary tract infections. Soothing to mucosa.

Expanded monograph available.

Cone Flower, Echinacea	*Echinacea sanguinea, E. purpurea, E. angustifolia*	Asteraceae

The *E. sanguinea* species is native and wild in east to north Texas; other species are non-native garden plants.

 Root and seed

 Fall

 Immunomodulatory, immunostimulant, antimicrobial, drawing

 Tincture 50-96% 1:2, fresh from over three year old roots.

No other uses noted.

Perennial wildflower with pinkish to whitish flowers, a very dark, prominent center with ray flowers drooping down around it. Grows 1-2 feet tall and tends to be rather striking.

All parts of this plant are used to tickle the immune system into responding. Internal and topical use against poisons, venoms, and to help the body to prevent or recover from infection. Draws poison out of the body.

It is best harvested after the third year of growth. Its populations in the wild are declining due to overharvesting for the herb market. Our native species is a no pick in the wild. You can harvest and replant the side pups of the root after harvest. Expanded monograph available.

Consumption Weed, Baccharis, Seep-Willow	*Baccharis neglecta*	Asteraceae

Native and weedy to Central and South Texas

 Leaves and stems

 Fall, when it flowers

Antimicrobial, calming, stomachic, antacid, antioxidant, astringent	*Perennial, semi evergreen, willow-like shrub with plumes of whitish flowers in the summer to early fall*
Infusion or decoction mostly noted with fresh young leaves	
Hedgerow or windbreak and soil stabilizer (37)	

Used for coughs, stomach irritability, heated conditions, spasmodic diarrhea (19), externally as a wound healer (38)

Studied in Mexico more than the U.S. Not a plant I use yet.

Copperleaf	*Acalypha radians, et al*	Euphorbiaceae

A. *radians* is native to Central and South Texas around waterways; species vary in distribution There are other species that grow in West Texas and Central Texas. I have only seen this one.

 Whole plant

 Spring

 Vulnerary, antifungal, internally cathartic laxative, antimicrobial, emetic, anodyne, expectorant (39)

Perennial to annual, low-growing herb with each sex of flower unique. Male flowers are tubular and female flowers are shorter with tiny leaflike growths.

 Aboveground parts infused in oil

No other uses noted.

Used in salves to treat wounds that won't heal. (18; 40) Some species specific to fungal infections (41).

Have not personally used in practice.

Cottonwood	*Populus deltoides*	Salicaceae

Native, common everywhere. Shade tree; usually grows near water.		
	Bark and, if exposed to a freeze, leaf buds	
	Bark in spring; leaf buds in winter (only exudes if exposed to freeze)	
	Analgesic, bitter, sedative	*One of the larger trees in Texas, with rustling, heart-shaped leaves and whitish cotton-like seeds that drift to ground like snow in spring*
	Dried bark or leaf buds infused in oil 1:5; tincture 96% 1:2 fresh	
Used by traditional peoples as a sacred communicator with spiritual realms. In Sundance ceremonies, a cottonwood pole is danced around as representation of the tree of life and the bark is given out as gifts. Like willow, it contains a rooting hormone and can be used to get other plants to put out roots (42).		

Pain reliever both topically and internally. Herbalist Michael Moore noted it to be more consistent in effectiveness than Willow.

In order to collect the leaf buds to make a nice oil, there needs to be freezing weather to get more resinous buds. Many parts of Texas are not cold enough for this. Expanded monograph available.

Country Mallow, Bala	Sida abutifolia, S. cordifolia, S. rhombifolia, et al	Malvaceae

Native weedy, opportunistic all over Texas, species dependent on area

 Root and aboveground parts

 Late summer to fall

 Some species sympathomimetic and many bitter. Diuretic, tonic, astringent, stimulant, rejuvenative, demulcent, emollient, antioxidant , anti-inflammatory

 Strong decoction or medicated milk; oil used topically

Some species have been used as a fiber for making twine, fishing lines, and rope in Africa, and as a potherb.

Annual to perennial erect groundcover herb with diamond shaped simple alternating leaves and creamy yellow five petaled flowers with stamens united around the pistil in a column

Some species, like *S. rhombifolia* and *S. cordifolia* (found in far south Texas) were found to have ephedrine-like compounds (useful during asthma attacks), but not all species necessarily have it. Other uses include neural pain and rebuilding of nervous system, cooling and calming. It is thought to balance all *doshas* in Ayurvedic medicine. *Bala* means balancing in Sanskrit.

I have not used this plant regularly in practice.

Cranesbill	*Geranium carolinianum*	Geraniaceae

Native, weedy; all over Texas, especially found in spring	
Aboveground parts	
Spring	
Astringent, styptic, antiseptic (43)	*Annual, hairy, ground-cover weed with pink flowers, unique fruit shaped like a bird's bill, and roundish, deeply dissected, blunt-toothed leaves with 5-7 lobes.*
Tea, infusion of aboveground parts	
One of the most common native wildflowers in North America (44). Is edible but not very tasty.	

Useful in helping to sooth burns and inflammations topically, diarrhea internally.

Similar to stork's bill. Have not used much in practice. Herbalist Jim McDonald uses one species of this plant frequently. (45)

Crepe Myrtle *Lagerstroemia indica*		Lythraceae
Non-native landscaping tree, currently not known to be invasive, joked to be the "official landscaping tree of Dallas"		
	Leaves	
	Summer	
	Astringent, hypoglycemic (46)	*Shrubby tree with shiny smooth, mottled trunks, simple opposite leaves, topped with long lasting showy clusters of crinkly crepe paper like pinkish flowers*
	Tea	*ornamental tree with smooth, graceful branches, topped with bright pink flowers in summer.*
Some species grown commercially for wood (47).		

Used in Philippines as a folk medicine to lower blood sugar in diabetics, seems to have effects similar to insulin (48) (49).

Have not personally used in practice.

Crossvine	*Bignonia capreolata*	Bignoniaceae

Native landscaping plant common in Central Texas		
	Flowers and leaves; root as an adaptogen	
	Spring to summer	
	Adaptogenic, alterative, antifungal, nervine	*Perennial, climbing, evergreen vine with bright trumpet-like drooping orange flowers, simple opposite leaves, and a long bean-like seedpod*
	None noted	
Also used for landscaping.		

Herbalist Matthew Wood references several folk healers in the southern U.S. who use it this to help strengthen the body (50). One citation says it is a substitute for sarsaparilla (51). May have some effect on the mind and cardiovascular system, as it contains resprine, an indole alkaloid. Species *B. capreolata* is related to others that treat fungal infections; may also have this property but no research has been done.

Have not used personally.

| Cucumber Pellitory | *Parietaria pensylvanica* | Urticaceae |

Wild, native, opportunistic

 Aboveground parts, especially leaves

 Spring

 The species *P. officinalis* is diuretic, refrigerant, laxative, slight demulcent (52).

Infusion, decoction

Edible and quite aromatic, nice cucumber flavor, especially young leaves, added to salads.

Herbaceous, annual weed, 6-8 inches tall with simple, smooth margined alternate leaves, the center stem usually covered with hairs and tiny greenish flowers. Forms stands.

Some species used to treat urinary tract stones, crystals, infections; trophorestorative to kidneys (53).

Common groundcover in Central Texas and Hill Country. Have eaten but not personally used in practice.

Wild, non-native, opportunistic; found in Central Texas, the Panhandle, and sporadically in a few other counties, especially in lawns

 All parts

 In Texas, late winter for tops; roots are not sizable enough to gather unless in a garden or north to east Texas

 Diuretic, alterative, refrigerant, hypoglycemic, nutritive

Herbaceous perennial with toothed, basal leaves forming a rosette hugging the ground from which spring solitary yellow blooms, one per stem, growing no more than 1 foot tall

 My preferred preparation is as a wine. Tincture 1:2, fresh whole plant 50% alcohol. Glycerite 100% 1:2, fresh.

Wine can be made from flowers, greens used as a potherb, very tasty and bitter. Roasted dandelion root may be used as a substitute for coffee.

Aboveground parts are full of minerals, and to increase urine flow. . Root used as a blood purifier to flush liver stagnation and signs of toxicity (cystic acne, etc.). Gentle, detoxifying, and regulating to hormones; balances kidneys and insulin. All parts bitter and regulating to digestion, especially tops.. Root is sweeter.

Common weed but often misidentified for many other dandelion-like plants. Make sure you know how to identify.. Expanded monograph available.

Desert Willow	*Chilopsis linearis*	Bignoniaceae

Native to West Texas; popular landscaping plant around central and south Texas		
	Leaves, bark, and flowers	
	Summer	

	Antifungal, antitussive, antimicrobial	*Perennial, shrubby, willow-like deciduous tree with pendulous pink flowers in summer and bean-like seedpods. Leaves are 5-12 inches long and linear. Tree can grow up to 20 feet tall.*
	Tincture 96% 1:2, fresh twigs, leaves and flowers	
Fiber, wood, food source— blossoms and seedpods (54)		

Used to treat fungal infections, candida (55), and respiratory in particular (56).

Shares the same family as pau d'arco and I have used similarly. Found to be very effective in treating folks with fungal lung infections in the common-ground free clinics in New Orleans after Hurricane Katrina.

Devil's Walking Stick	 *Aralia spinosa*	Araliaceae

Wild, opportunistic, native; found mostly in East Texas		
Root, bark, and berries		
Summer		
Expectorant, purgative tonic, alterative, berries are analgesic, diaphoretic, sialogogue (57)	*Evergreen, aromatic, perennial shrub. Spiny central stem is topped with large, pinnately compound leaves that create arrangements of white flowers ripening to purplish-black berries in fall. Can grow to 25 feet tall.*	
Traditionally, ointment		
No other uses noted.		

Used in folk medicine mostly as a purgative and alterative (58) to help cleanse.

This is the same family as the well-known medicinal, Ginseng. Some species of *Aralia* are used as an adaptogen for the respiratory tract, but there is no literature or folk use to verify that this species can be use, and in fact may be slightly toxic.

In historical literature, the plant is often confused with prickly ash (*Zanthoxylum*) (59). It may be that all of the references to Devil's Walking Stick being used as an analgesic for tooth pain are part of this confusion. I haven't tried it. When researching on your own, note that old sources may state uses for the wrong plant.

Dewberry	*Rubus trivialis*	Rosaceae

Wild, opportunistic, native to Central to North Texas	
Leaves and berries	
Spring	
Astringent (60), nutritive	*Perennial, white-flowered, prickly vine with trifoliate leaves, flowers produce tiny black berries. Can create dense mats of vines in some areas, prefers to be on a slight slope.*
Tea made from leaves or berries eaten fresh	
Berries are small and quite delicious. Maybe be used as a syrup, wine, or jam	

Leaves are a gentle astringent, good in teas as a reproductive and urinary tract tonic; root bark used to treat diarrhea.

May be used as a substitute for popular raspberry leaf (I have used as a tea). Beware of tiny thorns. I have never found enough of this plant to use consistently in practice, only for personal use.

Dogbane	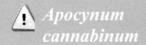 *Apocynum cannabinum*	Apocynaceae

Native; found more commonly in North Texas and the Panhandle to Far West

 Root—TOXIC

 Not noted

 Cardioactive (61)

Traditionally, decoction in very mediated doses

Perennial herb, grows 1-2 feet tall with reddish stems, white latex sap and clusters of small white flowers

Used as a phytoremediator against lead (62)

Used in small doses to help balance blood pressure relieve hypertension and edema (63)(swollen, boggy lymph (64)).

CAUTION: *Due to toxicity use only under the supervision of an experienced herbalist for drop-dosage emergencies.*

Elderberry	*Sambucus nigra, et al*	Caprifoliaceae

Native, more common in East Texas and Northeast Texas, sporadically in Central Texas

 Flowers and berries

 Flowers in spring, berries in late summer

 Antiviral, diaphoretic, expectorant, anti-inflammatory, berries nutritive, emollient, vulnerary (65)

I really like making a syrup or glycerite out of the berries. Fresh plant tincture of berries or flowers 50% alcohol 1:2

Jams, wines, liqueurs, juice, wood, dye

Perennial, shrubby tree with pinnately compound leaves and white clusters of flowers maturing into deep purple berries. Tends to form dense stands. .Leaves smell stinky, musky.

Used most commonly as support during cold and flu season against viral infections. Berries and flowers are used to help promote sweating and reduce coughing. Leaves were used in the preparation of the Green Elder Ointment, a folk remedy for bruises, sprains, chilblains, for use as a soothing wound healer. (66)

Elderberry fruits are an excellent source of anthocyanins, vitamins A and C, and a good source of calcium, iron, and vitamin B6 (67).

Elm	*Ulmus americana, et al*	Ulmaceae

Native to Central Texas, weedy

 Shaved outer bark of twigs and leaves

 Spring

 Demulcent, nutritive (*U. rubra*)

Cold extract of leaves and shaved twigs

Wood was planted as support for grapevines in winemaking (68).

Perennial, deciduous tree; simple leaves have doubly serrate margins to the edges; produces papery fruits called samaras

Soothing to mucous membranes in throat, stomach, and urinary tract (69). Especially helpful for dry ticklish throats.

I have taste tested the bark and leaves of the official "slippery elm" sold in commerce (*Ulmus rubra*) next to American and Cedar Elms. Mucilage is very similar, but flavor slightly sweeter in *U. rubra*. *Ulmus rubra* is on the United Plant Savers list of plants that may be in danger of being overharvested due to commercial pressure. (70)

Native, weedy, opportunistic; found all over Texas, but to a lesser degree south of the Panhandle

 Whole plant; root and aboveground parts in flower

 Spring

 Calming, antispasmodic, anti-inflammatory, nutritive

 I prefer the dried flowers in a tea.

Parts contain essential fatty acids, especially the seeds, which are produced commercially. The root was cooked and eaten at one time as a food.

Small, perennial wildflower with 4-petaled pink to yellow flowers, depending on species, and linear leaves that can form dense stands, growing no more than one foot high in the O. speciosa *species.*

Root is used as an antispasmodic, specifically for coughs (71). Herbalist Bridget Llanes taught me to use the flowers. They are used in teas to help regulate hormonal fluctuations and make menses more regular.

I use this plant a lot in remedies for women with reproductive complaints. Expanded monograph available.

False Gromwell	*Onosmodium bejerianse, O. helleri*	Boraginaceae

Native and common in Central Texas; otherwise sporadic in Texas, prefers to be in the forest understory	
Root	
Fall	
Diuretic, demulcent root	*Annual wildflower with whitish scorpioid blooms. Entire plant covered in bristly hairs. Leaves are linear with prominent venation and alternate down the stem, growing about 1.5 feet tall.*
Root decoction	
No other uses known.	

No modern use that I know of, but historical use for urinary tract and kidney complaints, edema (72).

It is noted in William Cook's *Physiomedical Dispensatory* that it may not be for long-term use and could exhaust the kidneys. (73) Has much more use in the homeopathic materia medica, but deserves a look at as an herb. (74) Reminds me very much of comfrey.

False Indigo	*Amorpha fruticosa*	Fabaceae

Native and common along waterways in more of the northerly half of the state	
Leaves, flowers, root	
Spring	
Contains flavonoids with unique antiviral activity (75)	*Perennial, graceful, deciduous shrub growing about 5 feet tall with soft even pinnate, compound leaves and showy purple flower spikes with yellow anthers that exude out flower spikes with yellow anthers that exude out.*
Tincture 100% 1:2, fresh root or leaves	
Also used as a dye (76)	

Used for summer colds and researched for use against HIV. (18) (77)

CAUTION: *Do not confuse with the toxic rattlebush, which looks alike and grows nearby!* Called *zisuihuai* in Chinese medicine (78).

Farkleberry	*Vaccinium arbutus*	Ericaceae

Native; common in central to eastern part of Texas		
Leaves and berries		
Berries ripen in summer		
Astringent, microcirculatory tonic, refrigerant, hypoglycemic	*Perennial, semi-evergreen, shrubby tree with white, bell-shaped clusters of flowers turning to grayish-blue berries. Can get up to 15 feet tall.*
Fresh leaves as an edible	
Edible berries, but not that great (kind of mealy tasting); can be made into jams, syrups, and wines. Leaves used to improve night vision. (79) (80)	

Nutritive, vascular support, regulates blood sugar. May be used as a tonic to strengthen capillaries in the extremities and eyes.

Uses of this plant come from its similarities to other *Vacciniums*. Bilberries, as they are called, may refer to more than one *Vaccinium*. I have taste tested the plant but have not used it in clinical settings yet.

Fennel	*Foeniculum vulgare*	Apiaceae

Non-native garden plant; has escaped in some parts of the Desert Southwest as a weed. Mostly grown in gardens in Texas.		
Whole plant; seed especially used medicinally		
Seeds in second year		
Carminative, galactagogue, hormonal, insect repellent, antispasmodic	*Biennial herb with yellow flowers and feathery basal leaves, very aromatic*	
Glycerite (preferred) 100% 1:2; tincture (secondarily) 50% 1:2		
Bulb commonly used as food; is one of the ingredients in absinthe		

Digestive spice used to help relieve gas and indigestion, encourage better milk flow (have had lots of success with moms for this), and is traditionally used to repel fleas. Also popularly used to relieve coughs and warm the lungs.

Grows easily in Central Texas and is a larval source for Black Swallowtail Butterflies, which may eat all the leaves, but I have never seen them kill it. Expanded monograph available.

Garlic	*Allium sativum*	Liliaceae/Amaryllidaceae/ Alliaceae

Non-native garden plant that can be grown well in Texas gardens

 Root (bulb)

 In many parts of Texas this may be planted in the fall and spring for harvests in spring and fall after tops die back.

Antioxidant, hepatoprotective, cardioprotective, cholesterolgenic, antimicrobial

 Fresh minced into food, or honey to make a syrup. Infused 1:4 into an oil.

Culinary spice, and to ward off "evil"

Herbaceous perennial producing sterile clusters of whitish flowers, tubular green stems, and long, linear, parallel-veined leaves.

Historical panacea for everything from heart disease, high cholesterol, liver diseases, infections, and parasites, both topically and internally. It is particularly popular in treating sore throats and yeast infections.

Heat can destroy some of its properties (81). Some people have allergies to it, and the juice has been known to create burns on people (82) (83). Expanded monograph available.

Giant Reed Grass, Nala	*Arundo donax*	Poaceae

Weedy and invasive; more common in Central, North, and East Texas, especially along waterways (84)	
Root	
None noted	

Psychoactive entheogen, emollient, diuretic, emmenagogic, hypertensive and hypotensive	*Tall, up to 20 feet, perennial bamboo-like grass with large seed heads flowering in late summer*
None noted	
Originally introduced to the U.S. as roofing material and erosion control. It is a candidate for biofuel. (85) Principle source of material for woodwind instruments. (86) Giant reed grass may also phytoremediate heavy metals like arsenic. (87)	

Have not used this in practice yet myself but the plant is a popular medicinal remedy from India and used internally and externally for skin inflammations, rashes, and herpes. It seems to also have a history of use for promoting menstruation and other fluids in the body. The plant has a very interesting pharmacology affecting the heart and would be interesting to investigate further.

Have no personal experience nor know anyone using this plant.

Ginger	*Zingiber officinale*	Zingiberaceae

Non-native garden plant can be grown in pots and moved inside if you live in areas that have hard freezes or planted in spring in shady, moist garden beds and dug up before freeze. Better production in South Texas.

 Root (rhizome)

 Dig roots in fall

 Antispasmodic, antioxidant (88), aromatic, analgesic, rubefacient, stimulant

 Tincture fresh 1:2 96%, dried 1:5 75%; decoction of root; powdered as a paste topically for pain and cramps. Lovely as a syrup, infuse in raw honey for several weeks then strain.

Tasty and popular as a ginger "beer"

Perennial, evergreen, tropical, reed-like stems with alternating long, linear, dark green leaves alternating and clasping around the stem terminating in a big bright, yellowish to red flower. Cultivars vary in color.

Used to help relieve gas pain and indigestion; promote better circulation, especially in digestive system; and relieve pain topically.

Easy to buy or grow. In Texas does well as a houseplant. Expanded monograph available.

Globe Berry, Watermelon Vine	*Ibervillea lindheimeri*	Cucurbitaceae

Native and common in South, Central, and West Texas		
Root		
None known		
Hypoglycemic (89)	*Deciduous, perennial vine with palmate leaves and green-striped fruits that turn bright red*	
None known		
No other uses known		

Some species from the Southwest are a traditional medicinal to treat diabetes by lowering blood sugar (90).

Have not used in practice

Globe Mallow, Desert Mallow	*Sphaeralcea ambigua*	Malvaceae

Native; more common in central to west Texas

 Aboveground parts

 Summer

 Demulcent, emollient

Cold tea/rinse

Makes a great hair rinse (91). Ceremonial use by some Native American tribes (92).

Perennial wildflower with arrangements of small orange, five-petaled flowers with a central column of stamens around the pistil. Furry, greenish-gray palmate leaves and stems. Can grow up to 2 feet tall.

All parts of this plant help soothe upset tummies and sore throats.

This plant tends to grow in drier parts of Texas, west of Austin.

Goldenrod	*Solidago nemoralis, et al*	Asteraceae

Native and weedy throughout Texas		
Aboveground parts in flower		
Blooms in fall in Texas		

Tonic, diuretic, astringent, antimicrobial	*Annual wildflower with pointed linear leaves almost seeming to spiral around the main stem. Can grow up to 6 feet tall. Topped with large panicles of nodding yellow flowers*
Tincture fresh 1:2 96%; dried as an infusion or tea. Used as an ointment by some herbalists.	
Contains rubber. Model T tires were made from goldenrod at one point (93). Dye plant.	

Used against urinary tract and/or kidney infections and as a preventative tonic for the urinary tract. Helps to mediate the effects of weepy, overproducing mucosa, whether it be the eyes, bladder, or nose. It can also be effective in treating symptoms associated with hay fever and allergies.

Has been misidentified as an allergen because it looks similar to ragweed, but its pollen is larger and heavier. Not much of an allergen itself.

Grapevine	*Vitis spp*	Vitaceae

Native and weedy throughout Texas, can even be invasive once established

Leaves and berries

Summer

Cardiotonic, nutritive, astringent, antioxidant

Tincture of leaves 1:2 fresh in 96% alcohol

Edible leaves and fruits, used as a wine or in jelly (94)

Perennial vine with grayish-green, palmate leave, small, inconspicuous arrangements of flowers that ripen to dark purplish-blue berries. Can get quite large and cover trees.

Used to help strengthen, tighten, and tone the cardiovascular system (95); the leaves alleviate insect bites and stings.

No other notes

Greenbrier	*Smilax bona-nox*	Smilaceae

Native, weedy, and invasive; throughout central to east Texas		
Rhizomes		
Spring for edible tips, late fall for rhizomes		
Adaptogen, alterative for kidneys	*Perennial, thorny vine; simple, heart-shaped, variable leaves with a shiny appearance, but often times have a white, mottled look; blue berries*	
Tincture or decoction		
Edible young leaves and tips. Root used to make root beer (96).		

The rhizomes of this plant can be used as a urinary and kidney tonic (97). It is a gentle alterative and may act to strengthen and tone the kidneys.

Difficult to harvest the rhizomes due to hard, packed soil in areas it grows, particularly clay and limestone. Good luck!

Gumweed	*Grindelia squarrosa, et al*	Asteraceae

Native, weedy; throughout Texas, especially south central to west

 Aboveground parts in flower

 Fall

 Expectorant, antispasmodic, antimicrobial, astringent

 Fresh tincture 96% alcohol 1:2

Dye plant (98). High amount of oil lends to its potential as a biofuel (99).

Annual wildflower growing about 1-2 feet tall with yellow, sticky flowers cupped in multiple layers of bracts and serrated, simple, almost glossy-looking leaves.

Respiratory infections, phlegm; humid, wheezy asthmatic conditions; and topically as an oil for poison ivy (100)

Expanded monograph available.

Hawthorne, Mayhaw	*Crataegus texana, et al*	Rosaceae

Native; located more commonly in East and North Texas. Mayhaw, found in swampy areas, is the most common.

 Berries and flowers

 Flowers in early spring and berries in late spring

 Hypotensive, cardiotonic

 Syrup 1:2 of berries; flowers in glycerin 1:2, fresh tincture 96% alcohol

Edible berries can be made into jellies and wines.

Shrubby tree covered in spines; small, variable leaves, arranged spirally in clusters along the stems, margins usually serrated; and white blossoms with multiple stamens, turning to red pomes

The berries and flowers of this tree are used to strengthen and tonify the heart, and to reduce high blood pressure.

Many of the Texas hawthornes are quite small, so don't look up when looking for this shrubby tree.

Henbit, Deadnettle	*Lamium amplexicaule*	**Lamiaceae**

Native, weedy; prolific in central to north and east Texas	
Whole plant	
Winter to spring	
Anti-inflammatory, gentle astringent	*Annual, ground-cover herb, growing 4-10 inches tall. Plant is erect, with terminal arrangements of pinkish or purplish flowers and opposite kidney-shaped leaves that directly clasp the stem. Entire plant is covered with tiny hairs.*
Dried plant infused in oil 1:5 or as tea	
Edible, tasty potherb. May be added fresh to salads.	

Aboveground parts act as a mild anti-inflammatory on skin which may be due to iridoid content along with compounds like quercetin. (101)

Too delicate to tincture. May be an analog plant to *Prunella vulgaris* (18). Can be misidentified as Ground Ivy (*Glechoma hederacea*). (102)

Holly, Yaupon, Possumhaw	*Ilex vomitoria, I. decidua*	Aquifoliaceae

Native; found in forests as a understory tree; mostly north, central and east Texas	
Leaves and bark	
None noted	

Stimulant	*Perennial, shrubby tree with white flowers, red berries, and smooth gray and white mottled bark.* I. vomitoria *is evergreen;* I. decidua *is deciduous. Leaves are small, simple, and oval-shaped with toothed margins.*
Tea of roasted leaves	
Historically, it was sold as Cassina or Cassina Tea (103), a stimulant in the Southeast U.S.	

Leaves and bark contain prominent amounts of caffeine and taste great. Caffeine may help to alleviate spasms and asthmatic responses, as well as migraines, so it may play a part in emergency first aid.

Berries may have the emetic effect that it gets its name from (*vomitoria*). Related to popular stimulant tea yerba mate, *Ilex paraguariensis*.

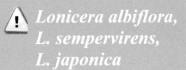

| Honeysuckle | ⚠ *Lonicera albiflora, L. sempervirens, L. japonica* | Caprifoliaceae |

Native and non-native varieties. The Japanese species (*L. japonica*) can be invasive. *L. japonica* and *L. sempervirens* are found mostly in the north, central, and eastern part of the state while *L. albiflora* is central to west.

 Flowers and leaves

 Spring

 Antimicrobial, antiviral, immune boosting, calming

 Tea

Also used in basketry (104).

Perennial, evergreen vine with irregular flowers ranging from white to yellow to pink. Leaves are opposite, simple, and oval in shape. Tendency to climb and cover other plants.

Honeysuckle is used for infections, heated conditions, and as a relaxant both internally and externally. It is particularly effective against viruses (105). I like to eat flowers while on hot Texas hikes to help me cool off.

Popularly used in traditional Chinese medicine. Beware of the toxicity potential of the berries in the Japanese variety.

Horehound	*Marrubium vulgare*	Lamiaceae

Weedy, non-native; widespread in south, central, and west Texas	
Aboveground parts	
Year round	

Bitter expectorant, vermifuge, antimicrobial, carminative, vulnerary	*Clumping, evergreen, perennial herb with grayish-silver leaves; grows erect up to 2 feet tall. Entire plant soft to touch due to downy hairs covering the plant. Leaves opposite, crinkled, and white flowers grow at intervals up the top part of the stem.*
It tastes best when infused into a syrup or made into candies	
Has been used as a tobacco substitute (106)and in place of hops in beer making.	

Used as a powerful expectorant and wound healer (107). Kills germs. May also be used to regulate digestion and relieve gas pains in the gut.

This plant is extremely bitter.

Horsetail	*Equisetum hyemale, et al*	Equisetaceae

Native; found near and in waterways	
Stems	
Spring through summer	
Nutritive, diuretic without altering electrolyte balance in body	*Ancient, segmented,dark green reed-like water plant with hollow stems.*
Tea or powdered and applied as a poultice	
Bioremediator; used to clean water. Also, broken up to scrub camping equipment, which is how it got one of its common names, scouring rush.	

This plant is extremely high in silica and most often used to help build bones or help resolve urinary tract infections where blood may be present (108). Popular in dental care.

Make sure you get the plant from clean waterways, since it can absorb toxins as it cleans the water.

Inmortal, Antelope Horns, Spider Milkweed  *Asclepias asperula* — Asclepiadaceae

Native; more common in west, north, and central Texas

 Root

 Summer

 Expectorant, oxytocin synergist, cardiotonic

 Tincture root 1:2 fresh 96%

Unopened pods can be eaten; they are esteemed as a pickled wild edible. (109)

Native perennial wildflower growing as a somewhat sprawling plant ending in striking white clusters of 5-petaled blooms with five stamens that have round white anthers in a ball shape, forming pods that burst open when ripe. Leaves are thick and oblong to lance-shaped along the stems.

Used to help break up and expel phlegm; help stalled labor contractions; and reduce enlarged, congestive hearts

Drop dosage; potentially toxic medicinal. Only to be gathered and used by experienced herbalists. Important plant for the monarch butterfly.

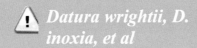
Mostly annual, shrubby herb with largish, simple leaves that are stinky and white. Trumpet-like blooms emit a lovely fragrance, more in the evening and night, later forming prickly pods of seeds.

 Leaves and blooms

 Fall (around Halloween) in Central Texas is when its bloom season is at its peak, and it can pop up all over the place. Visible at different stages at all times of the year from spring through fall. Dies back in freezes.

Sympathomimetic, antispasmodic, entheogenic

 Not recommended unless under the supervision of a knowledgeable and experienced herbalist.

Mostly annual, shrubby herb with largish, simple leaves that are stinky and white. Trumpet-like blooms emit a lovely fragrance, more in the evening and night, later forming prickly pods of seeds.

Bioremediator used to clean up nuclear radiation and heavy metals in soil (110) (111)

A very powerful, toxic plant that has been used to treat asthma attacks and spasming, painful muscles. In first aid situations, herbalist 7Song says the leaf can be puffed on once or twice to stop asthma attacks. Was a very popularly used plant by Eclectic physicians.

CAUTION: *Extremely toxic plant!* Must be used very carefully. If misused, can steal your soul, your sight, or your life. Seed pods are especially poisonous.

Jointfir, Mormon Tea, Ephedra	*Ephedra trifurca, E. antisyphilitica, et al*	Ephedraceae
Native and more common in West Texas desert communities		
Stems		
May be gathered throughout the year		
Nutritive, astringent, diuretic	*Perennial shrub with yellowish-green jointed stems forming large, clumping upright stands, producing small seeds that look like cones.*	
Tea		
Pleasant-tasting tea, where its common name Mormon tea came from		

The aboveground parts of this plant are high in minerals. Used to dry up and relieve allergies and treat kidney/urinary tract disorders.

Contains little, if any, of the controversial ephedrine and pseudoephedrine that Chinese ephedra (*Ma Huang*) has been known to contain (18).

Native, weedy and invasive; found all over Texas, from central to west more prolifically

 Leaves and berries medicinally

 Late winter/early spring is the preferred time to gather berries, but many trees produce throughout the year. Leaves may be gathered anytime.

 Aromatic, antimicrobial, rubefacient, astringent

 Tincture 1:2 of fresh berries at 96% or leaves infused into oil at 1:10

Culinary spice, traditionally used to flavor venison, and used in production of gin. Wood is soft but beautiful and used in nonstructural building. Leaves can also be dried and used as a smudge stick to clear the air.

Shrubby evergreen tree, needle-like leaves forming cones on male trees; bluish-purple berries on female trees. Entire plant highly aromatic; bark dark reddish brown and peeling.

Excellent as infused oil for topical use for cold arthritis (such as osteoarthritis) and sore muscles. Internally, it is used as a urinary tract antiseptic, but it can irritate kidneys, so please consult with an experienced herbalist prior to use. May also be used as a digestive aid, especially for protein digestion (18).

Can cause reddening of the skin as it draws circulation to an area. Some people are also *highly* allergic to the pollen, so much so that they are even affected by any part. Be careful and proceed with caution if this is the case. There is a big controversy over whether this tree is native and many people frown upon its water guzzling and clear it from land. Expanded monograph available.

Kidneywood, Palo azul	*Eysenhardtia texana*	Fabaceae

Native and common in Central to South Texas	
Twigs and leaves	
Intermittent blooms, most vibrant in the fall but may be gathered throughout spring and summer	
Astringent, antimicrobial	*Shrubby deciduous tree with small, pinnately compound leaves that have a greasy orange smell. Produces white blooms and pea-like pods. Bark is smooth.*
Tincture of woody parts with leaves 75% 1:2, fresh	
Attracts pollinators butterflies	

Some species used to treat urinary and kidney infections (112)

I first heard about its folk use from some herbalists in Arizona. I then did research and found a common species in Mexico, *E. polystachyma*, used to treat kidney infection. Since then I began using it for my own clients with success.

Lamb's Quarters, Epazote	*Chenopodium album, C. ambrosioides, et al*	Chenopodiaceae

Native weedy species (Lamb's Quarters) and garden varieties with more aromatics (Epazote).

 Leaves

 Late spring to summer, even into fall

 Weedy species *C. ambrosioides* is nutritive. Garden species, such as *C. ambrosioides*, used as a carminative and vermifuge.

 Potherb, if it's *C. album*, or add powdered leaves of *C. ambrosioides* as a pinch of spice to beans.

Some tribes used Lamb's Quarters flowers ground up as a flour (113).

Annual herb 1-6 feet tall and can become bushy in appearance. Variable leaves and stems are light blue-green to striped with purple. Leaves alternate down the stem shaped from ovate to lanceolate with irregular margins. Flowers are small and yellowish green.

C. album used mainly as nourishment. *C. ambrosioides*, the garden species is added to meals to prevent gas, also used in some parts of Mexico to kill parasites in the digestive tract.

Edible species has some oxalates that can irritate kidneys if too much of the raw herb is consumed.

Lantana	⚠ *Lantana horrida*	Verbenaceae

Native, weedy, found wild all over South and Central Texas	
Leaves and flowers	
Summer, in bloom period, into fall	
Antimicrobial (114), vulnerary, counterirritant, stomachic, diaphoretic	*Perennial, deciduous shrub with clusters of multicolored flowers, usually pink, yellow and white, forming purplish-blue, berry-like fruits; leaves aromatic with bright, green scent, simple, oval, and can be rough like sandpaper.*
None personally noted, but tea or tincture may be appropriate, even oil.	
May be a good insect repellent	

Has a history of use for digestive complaints. Can be used topically on wounds. Some species have been used to treat colds and flu symptoms (115). Herbalist Sam Coffman uses this in practice.

May be somewhat toxic, especially seeds. I have gotten contact dermatitis from the plant. (116)

Leatherstem	*Jatropha dioica, et al*	Euphorbiaceae

Native to West Texas deserts and South Texas plains

 Stems

 May be gathered throughout the year

 Antimicrobial, vulnerary

 Fresh sap applied to wounds

Some species of this genus are being looked at as a source of biofuel, and some have been used as a jet fuel! (117)

Perennial shrub with arching, reddish flexible stems; small, simple alternating leaves; and drooping, whitish, urn-shaped flowers along the ends of the stem. Male and female flowers on the same shrub.

The fresh sap from members of this genus (especially from Brazilian rain forests) is used as a first aid remedy for cuts and scrapes to seal and prevent infection.

Have not tried our species.

Lemon Balm, Melissa	*Melissa officinalis*	Lamiaceae

Non-native common garden plant; does well central to east and north Texas in shade gardens

 Aboveground parts

 Spring and fall. If you cut it back it will produce a second bloom.

Antiviral, diaphoretic, calming

 Tea or tincture fresh 96% 1:2

Also used as an infused wine. Attracts bees!

Herbaceous, perennial, clumping ground cover with simple, opposite leaves, producing tiny white flowers. Crushed leaves smell like a very sweet lemon.

Mood elevating, great tasting, and helpful in treating viral infections. Also seems to affect the thyroid, resolve headaches, and is used topically to help prevent and resolve herpes outbreaks.

Common European garden herb I find essential to my practice. Expanded monograph available.

Loquat	*Eriobotrya japonica*	Rosaceae

Non-native; common landscaping plant in Central Texas

 Fruit and leaves

 Late spring when they fruit

 Antispasmodic, antioxidant, chemopreventative, sedative (118)

Syrup of fruit and tea of leaves

Edible fruits

Perennial, evergreen tree with large, simple, dark-green, glossy leaves forming large clusters of round, soft fruits.

Popular cough remedy in China (leaves), but the fruits also seem to act as a sedative. Leaves are being used in cancer research (119).

As with all rose family plants, including apples, don't chew on a lot of seeds as they have some amount of cyanide in them.

Madrone	*Arbutus xalapensis*	Ericaceae

Native, infrequent, and spotty distribution in Hill Country bioregion, more prolific in West Texas

 Leaves

 Leaves can be gathered year round

 Antiseptic, astringent

 Tincture fresh 1:2 75%

Evergreen, perennial, shrubby tree with a graceful appearance; red, peeling bark; and simple, oval, tough, leathery leaves with white, bell-shaped flowers turning to red berries

Fruit is edible, and in Portugal and Spain it is distilled into popular alcoholic beverages, one of the names being *Medronho* (120).

Useful in the treatment of urinary tract infections and soothing inflamed skin

Can be used interchangeably with other *Arbutus* species, uva ursi and manzanita.

Magnolia	*Magnolia grandiflora*	Magnoliaceae
Non-native landscaping tree, found more in the north and east of Texas		
Bark and flowers		
Spring/fall for bark, spring for flowers		
Bitter, stimulant, antimicrobial		*Tall, perennial, evergreen tree with simple, leathery, glossy, green leaves producing large white fragrant blooms with 6-12 petals forming into a rose colored ovoid fruit*
None noted		
In Japan the leaves are used to wrap food or as cooking vessels.		

Mainly used in traditional Chinese and Japanese medicine (121). Magnolia bark has been explained by herbalist Will Morris to regulate the Vital Force, especially liver and spleen, drain blood lymph, and open the diaphragm. Also helps those who have problems speaking the truth, as if there is a plum pit in the throat. It helps those who have passive-aggressive tendencies to be able to be better communicators.

Have not gathered yet in my practice

Mesquite	*Prosopis glandulosa*	Fabaceae

Native and invasive due to degradation of land by cattle ranches. It is one of the few trees that cattle won't eat, so it is extremely prolific in rangeland. Found all over Texas but more in the western half of the state.

 Leaves, pods, bark, and beans

 Depends on part used. Leaves and pods in spring, bark in fall (only from small side branches—never debark a trunk!)

 Anti-inflammatory, astringent, nutritive, hypoglycemic, hypotensive

 Isotonic solution of the tea as an eye wash

Edible beans and pods are high in protein, can be made into a meal and added to flours. The pods can be made into a syrup. This spiny tree has a long history of use as a food source and medicine.

Perennial deciduous, shrubby tree with dangling, double-compound, dissected leaves. Drooping yellowish-white flowers produce bean pods. Tree is covered in large spines.

May be used as a gentle anti-inflammatory to soothe eye infections and skin inflammation, and to assist in lowering blood sugar and blood pressure

Have only briefly experimented with this topically as a poultice to relieve inflammation. A lot of the literature of traditional and tribal use revolves around eyes. (122)

107

Milkwort	*Polygala alba, P. lindheimeri*	Polygalaceae

Native; infrequent and spotty distribution, more easterly in Texas than west, throughout the Hill Country

 Root

 Spring to summer

Bitter, aromatic, expectorant, antispasmodic	*Delicate, slender, perennial wildflower topped with small white flower arrangements. Easy to overlook. Grows about a foot tall in open fields.*
Fresh tincture 1:2 96%, small frequent doses	
No other uses known	

Used to treat lung infections, coughs (123)

I have never run into enough of this to actually harvest. It's a good plant to know about as historically used, but may not be the best choice for wild harvest. In Chinese medicine it is known as *yuan zhi*, (124) and is a popularly used plant.

Mimosa, Silk Tree	*Albizia julibrissin*	Fabaceae

Non-native landscaping plant found from central to east and North Texas. Gets larger as you move east.

 Small stems and branches, flowers

 Flowers in summer, bark from small branches may be collected spring or fall

 Topical—vulnerary, emollient, antimicrobial. Internal—calming, sedative, anodyne

Perennial, deciduous tree with compound, pinnate leaves and poofy, fragrant bright pink flowers turning into pea like pods.

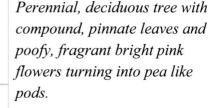

 Extract of fresh blossoms 1:5, 2.5 96% alcohol; 2.5 100% glycerin. Tea of flowers. Have not used bark.

No other uses known.

This is a popular traditional Chinese medicinal plant, used to nourish the spirit and relieve the mind from anxiety and tension. Bark more often used to treat the physical rather than emotional or spiritual body (125).

The name of this plant used in traditional Chinese medicine is *he huan hua*.

Mint	*Mentha arvensis, M. piperita, M. spicata, et al*	Lamiaceae

Native, many non-native cultivars are also available.	
Aboveground parts	
Spring, cut back and comes back in late summer	
Aromatic, antimicrobial, stimulant, diaphoretic, antispasmodic, carminative	*Herbaceous, spreading, creeping perennial herb with simple, opposite leaves and square stems. Crushing the leaves creates a fresh minty smell.*
It makes a very pleasant tea.	
Culinary as a flavoring	

The aboveground parts of mint may be used as a antimicrobial wash, insect repellent, to calm spasms internally and externally, soothe upset stomachs, or help you break a fever through stimulating perspiration and sweating.

The name of this plant in Chinese medicine is *bo he* (126). Expanded monograph available.

Motherwort	*Leonurus cardiaca, L. siberica*	Lamiaceae

Non-native, enthusiastic garden plant. *L. siberica* species can get invasive.	
Aboveground	
Blooms and is at peak in summer	
Antispasmodic,emmenagogue, diaphoretic, calming, cardiotonic	*Herbaceous, clumping perennial with square stems; opposite, incised leaves, and pinkish flowers in whorls around stem at intervals.*
Fresh tincture at 1:2 96%	
There are stories of using the plant in body care formulas for the skin in China (127). No other uses noted.	

Calming to the nervous system and tonifying to cardiovascular system. Traditionally used for many symptoms related to hormonal imbalance in women (128) (129). *L. siberica* has a history of use in a similar vein and now has some sort of fad recognition for being entheogenic.

I became very impressed with this herb when I had one self-seed under a rose bush, never get watered, and grow big and healthy in the middle of a Texas summer. For this, it deserves recognition.

Native, with different species scattered throughout the state. *M. microphylla* more to the west and *M. rubra* more to the east.

 Leaves and fruit

 Berries in late spring

 Demulcent, berries used to "build blood," cardiovascular tonic, leaves emollient and hypoglycemic (130), bark anthelmintic

 Syrup of leaves and berries

Deciduous shrubby tree with simple, sandpapery leaves, and ,elongated edible berries, dark purple when ripe, some species have white berries.

Edible berries, great as wine or preserves. White mulberry leaves are used as feedstock for silkworms in China (131).

Berries soothe respiratory infections and coughs, nourish the blood. Leaves are more alterative, shift the body out of illness. Bark used to expel parasites. (132) Popular use for sore throats and coughs. Leaves and root bark have reported effects against high blood sugar and are used to treat diabetes.

Have seen the tree become diseased and the fruits inedible due to some sort of fungus that causes the tree's fruit to explode outward and almost look like popcorn.

Mullein	*Verbascum thapsus*	Scrophulariaceae

Non-native, weedy, all over the U.S. and Texas

 Whole plant

 Flowering is dependent on many factors. I have seen it actively shooting up flower stalks mainly in spring, but not always.

Anti-inflammatory, expectorant, astringent, demulcent	*Biennial herb with basal rosette of soft, simple, elongated, grayish-green, downy leaves that shoot up a column of yellow flowers in the second year along the stem.*
Fresh tincture 1:2 at 96% and as a dried plant oil 1:5	
As tinder for fire; the flower stalk has been used as a torch	

Leaves have popular use as a soothing tonic to the mucosal lining of our bodies and skin, and to help heal lung and urinary tract ailments. The flowers are often steeped in oil and used for earaches. Herbalists are also experimenting with it topically for use in joint inflammation and pain, especially along the spine.

Expanded monograph available.

Popular and planted as landscaping shrub, extremely invasive in Central Texas. Do not plant; can escape into wildlands.

 Twigs

 None Noted

 Alterative, antimicrobial

 Topical use only. Decoct as a wash on infected areas of the body or as a salve.

Evergreen shrub growing about 3-4 feet tall with white flowers forming red berries. Leaves are compound, pinnate turning reddish.

Traditionally, this was planted around the home to ensure good dreams and chase away nightmares, and the wood was used as toothpicks (133). Interestingly, a compound called nantenine in the plant may have been found to block the effects of the street drug MDMA (134).

Suggest sticking to topical use due to controversial toxicological views on this plant. Studies have shown good documentation of antifungal compounds in wood.

POTENTIAL TOXICITY. Controversial in toxicity, berries may be too poisonous for use but does have some historical use of woody parts used internally. Also, just because one of the compounds could be helpful for someone in a drug-induced state, that doesn't mean that making them a tea of this and giving it to them would work..

114

Nettles	*Urtica chamaedryoides*	Urticaceae

Native, wild; found in shaded woodlands more in the southern part of the state	
Whole plant	
Early spring	
Astringent, tonic to the urinary tract, nutritive	*Annual herb growing about 1 foot tall with simple, opposite, heart-shaped leaves, square stems, and visible stinging hairs. Flowers are tiny, white and inconspicuous.*
Tea	
As a wild edible green. Upon cooking, the stinging hairs are no longer active.	

Young leaves are a great nutritive tea, high in many minerals, especially iron and calcium. Herbalist Kiva Rose has written that the seed may be restorative to those suffering from adrenal exhaustion, and the root of some species is used to treat enlarged prostates. The plant has been used as a urinary tract tonic and in helping to treat urinary tract infections. It has been found to have a slight antihistamine response in the body.

CAUTION: *This plant will sting if it isn't touched gently and with intent.* Rather than foraging this plant in the wild, please cultivate it in gardens or we will lose it as a wild edible. Older plants have higher levels of oxalates, which could irritate kidneys. Ours are so short-lived, I doubt they have enough time to develop high levels of oxalates.

Native; many species, prolific throughout the state

 Bark and leaves

 Depends on species; when new leaf growth is abundant

 Astringent

Deciduous or evergreen tree. Rough, deeply grooved bark on main trunk; trunks can get quite thick. Leaves are simple to incised or lobed, and a bit glossy. Produces acorns in the fall.

 Leaves and twigs in tincture, fresh 1:2 50%; or as a decoction made into a topical wash

Edible nuts if prepared properly

Bark and leaves are used as an astringent topically to help tonify, dry out, and soothe inflammations, especially in the mouth, throat, and traditionally to stop diarrhea. May use topically like witch hazel on spider veins and bug bites. May be too drying internally, so stick to external use.

Too drying for use as tea internally. May hurt your tummy because the tannins are so strong.

Ocotillo	*Fouquieria splendens*	Fouquieriaceae

Native to the deserts of West Texas		
Outer bark		
None noted		
Lymphatic stimulant		*Unique perennial shrub with spindly, grayish, thorn-covered limbs shooting up from the ground in a rosette towards the sky. Leafs out briefly after rain with brilliant red flower production.*
Fresh bark in tincture at 96% 1:2		
Considered a very spiritually significant plant. It is said that you should seek it out to meditate beneath. It is also used as a living fence material in West Texas.		

Outer bark used to treat pelvic congestion and lymphatic stagnation. Particularly helpful with epididymitis and edema from PMS

This will grow fine as a xeriscape plant as far east as Austin (I've never seen it further east than that). If you do choose to harvest, cut one limb at base, do not cut several ends of branches. In desert bioregions arid plants need less injury sites to heal from harvest.

Old Man's Beard, Scarlet Leatherflower	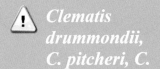 *Clematis drummondii, C. pitcheri, C. texensis, et al*	Ranunculaceae

Native; found more commonly in the southern and western half of the state	
Aboveground parts in flower	
Spring to summer for *C. pitcheri*, *C. drummondii* in summer to early fall	
Calming, analgesic	*Toxic perennial vines with showy, pink, purple, or white flowers.* C. texensis *is an endemic no pick (cultivate only).*
Fresh plant tincture 96% at 1:2	
Ornamental as landscaping plants	

Some members of this genus are used to treat migraines. Need more research on Texas species due to potential toxicities. This is for emergency use only in very small amounts

CAUTION: *Drop dosage. Use only under the supervision of an experienced practitioner.* This plant has highly toxic constituents and must be used properly in the correct dose. Is extremely irritating and blistering to mucosa and skin.

| Passionflower | *Passiflora incarnata, P. foetida, P. affinis, P. lutea, et al* | Passifloraceae |

Native and non-native varieties grow prolifically. Native varieties found in the wild more to the south and central parts of Texas.

 All aboveground parts, especially leaves

 Most prolific in late summer and fall

 Calming, sedative, sudorific

 Tincture fresh at 50% 1:2, or drink as a tea. Glycerite is also very nice

Edible fruit. Great landscaping plant. Host to Gulf fritillary butterfly.

Perennial vine with simple, lobed leaves and showy, very unique solitary flowers in varying colors and sizes. I like to think of the plant as "alien" in appearance.

Use primarily to treat anxiety and help promote sleep. May also calm heart palpitations brought on by stress.

The non-native garden varieties grow prolifically in yards and gardens. Unless you are in East Texas, most native varieties are very small and fragile, found in small amounts, and not worth trying to harvest as medicine. Expanded monograph available.

Peach Tree	*Prunus persica*	Rosaceae

Non-native landscaping plant that can be grown in most parts of the state, though the eastern half of the state is easier, due to lack of water to the west.

 Leaves and fruit

 Spring to summer

 Refrigerant, stomachic, antinausea, bitter

Deciduous tree with elongated, dangling, simple leaves in clusters, pink flowers, and produces orange to red, edible fruit.

 Cordial with fruit and leaf or tincture of leaf 1:2 fresh 50%

Absolutely delicious edible fruits

The leaf especially is used to help cool off when you are overheated; seems to affect both the digestive and cardiovascular systems as far as reducing heated conditions in the body. Alleviates nausea. Herbalist Matthew Wood lists this as one of his 10 most indispensable herbs.

May not want to consume large amounts of the dried leaf. There is concern in this family over the cyanogenic glycosides which may be potentially toxic in the dried leaf or the pits of the fruits.

Pennyroyal	*Hedeoma drummondii, H. acinoides*	Lamiaceae

Native; grows in open, sunny fields, found in Central Texas; *H. drummondii* extending West	
Mostly aboveground parts	
Spring	
Alterative, antimicrobial, carminative, diaphoretic, emmenagogue	*Low-growing, annual to perennial wildflower only getting about 6 inches tall with tiny pinkish flowers, opposite minute leaves; sweet lemony smell when leaves are crushed.*
Fresh tincture 1:2 at 75%	
Has a history of use as a bug repellent	

Aboveground parts can be used some of the same ways as Common European Pennyroyal—as a uterine tonic and blood mover, promoting menstruation, when stalled. Helps relieve fevers through sweating. Aromatics may also be useful in killing pathogens (135).

Do not confuse this plant with the European variety's essential oil that has some controversy historically, when it was misused and drank as an abortifacient. Drinking any essential oil is extremely dangerous and toxic. In this case, someone died from ingestion and all pennyroyal products were taken off the market for a time.

Peppergrass	*Lepidium virginicum*	Brassicaceae

Common native weed found all over fields and empty lots	
Aboveground parts	
Late spring to summer	
Aromatic, expectorant, stimulant, antimicrobial, counterirritant, vermifuge	*Annual to short-lived-perennial herb with basal rosette of oblong leaves with toothed margins, stem a bit hairy. Small, spirally arranged, inconspicuous flowers around the main stem producing flat, roundish seeds with notch at tip.*
None known	
Also used as a culinary spice	

Used to treat parasites and dysentery in Mexico. In Asia and the Middle East, it is used for respiratory complaints. Currently it is under study for its potential use in opening bronchial passageways during asthma attacks (136).

Have not used this yet in my practice.

Persimmon	*Diospyros texana*	Ebenaceae

Native; mostly south and central parts of Texas, moves a bit west into the Rio Grande Valley	
Fruit	
Early fall for fruits	
Diuretic, astringent	*Perennial, semi-evergreen shrub with very smooth bare trunks, simple, ,small, tough, oval leaves and small, round, green hairy fruits ripening to blackish in color.*
Oil extraction of green fruits for salve	
Edible fruits particularly good as a wine or jam	

Used topically in a green fruit salve and internally as a diuretic that contains potassium.

Green fruit salve of persimmon is a traditional Appalachian folk remedy. Haven't tried it yet with our species.

Periwinkle	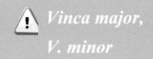 *Vinca major, V. minor*	Apocynaceae

Non-native, weedy and invasive landscaping plant

 Mostly synthesized into drugs

 None noted due to toxicity

 Calming, sedative, tonic

 Topically as a sedative

No other uses known.

Evergreen, creeping groundcover with opposite, solitary leaves that are tough, leathery and glossy. Produces five petaled purple flowers.

Made into drugs (high in alkaloids) used in Alzheimer's and cancer research (137). It is full of toxic alkaloids so internal use is discouraged. May be used topically to help relax cramping.

This plant is synthesized into use as a drug. Due to potential toxicities, internal use is discouraged. (138)

Plantain	*Plantago lanceolata, P. virginica, et al*	Plantaginaceae

Native and non-native, weedy; found all over North America and Texas in waste spaces, abandoned lots, and the sides of trails. Native varieties are also found in open fields.

 Whole plant

 Spring

 Astringent, demulcent, tonic, antimicrobial, antifungal

 Tincture 1:2, fresh aboveground parts at 50% or fresh leaf chewed up and applied topically as a poultice on wounds

Seed husks from this plant genus are used as a source of fiber and sold commercially as psyllium. The plant is full of minerals like calcium and has also been used as a wild edible or in preparations for its nutritive value.

Annual to perennial hairy herb forming basal rosette of linear leaves shooting up a spike of tiny, inconspicuous flowers. Native varieties in Texas have small, linear leaves with soft hairs covering them.

Leaves are an especially useful first aid remedy to soothe abrasions and stop bleeding. It can be used to help relieve tickles in the throat and kill infections internally and topically. Plantain became one of my favorite fire ant bite remedies, thanks to Alexa Villalobos from Fertile Ground Landscaping, and is effective against contact dermatitis from a variety of other prickly Texas plants.

Folk name for European variety is "white man's foot" as it followed colonists, so it makes sense that it heals an area after it has been disrupted. This is not related to the plantain sold at the grocery store that looks like a banana.

Pleurisy Root, Butterfly Weed	*Asclepias tuberosa*	Asclepiadaceae

Native; found more east and seems to thrive in our sandy soils rather than clay-based

 Root

 Summer to fall

 Expectorant, anti-spasmodic, diaphoretic

 Tincture of the root fresh 1:2 96%

Plant it to provide food for Monarchs

Perennial herb with pointed, linear leaves alternating around a main stem, topped with a cluster of brilliant orange flowers. Grows about 1 foot tall.

Used to treat respiratory infections that are stuck deep in the lungs and to relax painful, spastic coughs

This is a no-pick in the wild and rather hard to cultivate unless soil is amended properly. The plant is an attractant for monarch butterflies and is being watched by United Plant Savers as a plant that is threatened in the wild from overharvesting. Best to try to propagate. There is a South American species *Asclepias curassavica* often incorrectly labeled at garden shops all over Central Texas as *A. tuberosa*, or butterfly weed. The species looks very different from our native variety, so make sure when purchasing you are getting the correct species. This family has too many potential toxicities to experiment with different species.

Poke	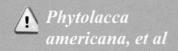 *Phytolacca americana, et al*	Phytolaccaceae

Weedy and can be invasive. Found all over forested areas as an understory plant, more from the central to eastern parts of Texas.

 Root

 Fall

 Lymphatic alterative

 Root tincture 1:10 96%

Leaves are prepared by washing several times and eaten as a potherb.

Perennial herb, some species growing 10 feet tall. Large, simple leaves. Plant is topped with large clusters of white flowers turning into showy, dark-purple berries in the summer to fall.

Applied both topically and internally to swelling and lumps to help drain lymphatic congestion from an area. Has a history of use on lumps and cancerous growths and seems to have an affinity to glands associated with reproductive tissue.

Toxic botanical. Must be used properly and not recommended for harvest unless properly trained and knowledgeable of the medicinal applications.

Prairie Tea	*Croton monanthogynus*	Euphorbiaceae

Native and abundant; especially throughout the central part of the state and Rio Grande Valley

 Aboveground parts

 Late Summer

 Aromatic, diuretic

 Tea

Used mostly as a popular tea. Yum!

Annual herb reaching about 2 feet tall and 3 feet wide. Somewhat flat topped in appearance, leaves usually alternate, small, up to 2 inches in length, and an aromatic, almost sweet smell. Flowers are either male or female, and so appear different.

No known medicinal uses.

Make sure to identify the proper species, as this genus has some other members that can be too toxic to use as a tea (139).

Prairie Vervain	*Glandularia bipinnatifida*	Verbenaceae

Native; found all over Texas in open fields and along the sides of washes, especially roadsides, in full sun

 Aboveground parts in flower

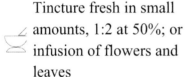 May have several bloom cycles throughout the year, the cold snaps will finally make it die back

 Diaphoretic, bitter, sedative

Tincture fresh in small amounts, 1:2 at 50%; or infusion of flowers and leaves

Landscaping, xeriscaping plant. There is much magical use and folklore surrounding the use of Vervain as a protective amulet to banish evil (140).

Perennial, clumping wildflower with pinnately compound, deeply dissected leaves, growing around a foot tall with purple clusters of flowers. As the plant ages it reaches towards the sun and gets taller and more spindly.

Provides both glandular support and calms hot, irritated, nervous conditions in the body. May be used as first aid support for those suffering from irritable bowel syndrome and fluttery feelings in the stomach leading to gastric distress. Historically used to bring about a sweat to help cool the body from fever and heat.

This plant was recently split out of the *Verbena* genus. Expanded monograph available.

Prickly Ash	*Zanthoxylum clava-herculis, Z. hirsutum*	Rutaceae

Native *Z. clava-herculis* found in Central Texas through to East Texas; *Z. hirsutum* stays more central. Easterly specimens seem to grow taller.

 Berries and bark

 Summer

 Stimulant, antimicrobial, analgesic, antiparasitic, digestive, bitter

 Tincture of berries, leaves, and twigs 1:2 at 96%

Used as a spice in Szechuan cooking

Perennial. Grows as a shrubby tree covered in small spines and pinnately compound leaves. Creates clusters of berries in the summer. Fresh citrus scent and tingly taste.

Used to treat pain, especially tooth pain and prickly neural pain in extremities. Aids in circulation. Chinese medicine uses it as an aid against parasites.

Historical writings on this plant confuse *Aralia spinosa* with *Zanthoxylum spp*, so be very careful when doing research. Expanded monograph available.

Prickly Pear, Nopal	*Opuntia lindheimeri, O. wrightii, et al*	Cactaceae

Native, weedy; all over Central to West Texas, preferring full sun and open fields

 Stems, flowers, fruits

 Pads throughout the year, berries in fall

 Astringent, nutritive, antioxidant, insulin regulating, cardiotonic, demulcent, hydroscopic

 As a cordial from the fruit, glycerite from the flower 100%, or tincture of the fruit or flowers 1:2 at 96%. Juice of Pads.

The fruits and pads can be carefully prepared and eaten after spines are burned off or otherwise removed. The pads are most often found pickled and are delicious with eggs. The fruits can be carefully stripped of prickles and eaten raw, made into jelly, or a wonderful wine. May be sliced open and used as a sort of canteen.

Shrubby succulent with modified, jointed stems called pads, usually covered in long and short spines and gorgeous showy flowers in yellow to orange hues turning to red tunas (fleshy fruits).

Medicinally, the inside of the pads contains mucilage used to help soothe burns and abrasions. The pads and fruit can be juiced to help stabilize blood sugar and are commonly used in the Southwest U.S. and Mexico in this way. The juice can also act as a laxative. Powdered innards of pads make a great wound powder.

Expanded monograph available.

| Prickly Poppy |  **⚠ *Argemone aurantiaca, A. albiflora, A. mexicana*** | **Papaveraceae** |

Native; found in Central Texas and more to the south and westerly parts of the state	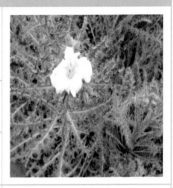
Aboveground parts and buds	
Late spring and summer	
Calming, analgesic, anthelmintic, expectorant	*Annual erect wildflower with delicate white or yellow flowers atop grayish-blue, prickly foliage getting almost 3 feet tall.*
Smoke dried flower buds, just a puff, otherwise not used much due to potential toxicity.	
No other uses known.	

Aboveground flowering parts and pods used as a pain reliever; herbalist Michael Moore has folks smoke the pods to take the angst out of withdrawal from marijuana addictions. In Ayurveda, it is known as *satyanashi* and has a history of use against parasites. The tribes of North America had many ways to prepare this, especially externally.

Full of alkaloids, some toxic. The oil was found as an adulterant in India and caused a lot of poisonings (141). Not recommended for use.

Purslane	*Portulaca oleracea, P. mundula*	Portulacaceae

Weedy, now thought to be native. Comes up as a ground cover at various times of the year in open fields and abandoned lots throughout the state with a very long bloom cycle, especially in drier times. Found more in the southern and western parts of the state.

 Aboveground and seeds

 Depends on rain and temperature, but normally found in fall in Central Texas and is sometimes known to be quite prolific throughout the year

 Refrigerant, nutritive, vulnerary, analgesic, anti-inflammatory

Eat it raw in Salads! Fresh poultice or fresh juice

Edible wild plant high in essential fatty acids, vitamins A and C, and minerals (142) (143)

Prostrate, clumping, succulent, annual ground cover with simple, opposite leaves and reddish stems making small, brightly colored flowers, usually yellow or pink depending on variety and area.

Cooling to hot conditions in the body, hydrocolloids help to heal wounds and stop bleeding; also full of alkaloids that assist in relieving pain and inflammation

No other notes

Queen of the Meadow  *Stillingia texana*	Euphorbiaceae

Native; found more in the Panhandle, east and coastal parts of Texas into Central Texas

 Root

 Fall

Lymphatic stimulant, secretory

Tincture of fresh root in small doses 1:2 96%

No other uses known.

Perennial, herbaceous wildflower with inconspicuous spikes of yellowish flowers at the tips. Grows up to 1 foot tall. Leaves are leathery, cool to the touch, lance shaped, and attached directly to the main stem in whorl-like arrangements. Breaking the stem produces white latex.

Used when there is lingering illness or tissues that have lymph stagnation, as in poorly resolving infections, etc.

TOXIC: *Do not use aboveground parts.* Traditional use is in small, frequent doses of 10 drops or so.

Ragweed	*Ambrosia trifida, A. artemisiifolia, et al*	Asteraceae

Native, weedy; various species found more towards the north, east, and southern side of the state with some areas of Central Texas having some as well. Not too prolific, but common.

 Leaves and flowers

 Summer

 Bitter, antihistamine, antimicrobial, stimulant, aromatic

 Tincture of fresh plant without flowers present 1:2 96%

Also used as a dye.

Mostly annual to perennial herb up to 20ft tall with bright-green, trifoliate leaves up to 1 foot in length. Other species tend to be shrubbier with doubly pinnate, dissected leaves. All are very aromatic and weedy. Small, inconspicuous, yellow-green arrangements at tops. Color can range in species; some have silvery leaves.

Can be used to relieve hay fever, congestive asthma from allergies and as a decongestant. Herbalist Benjamin Zappin uses this regularly in his clinic.

Common allergen to some and may cause severe reactions. If worried about that, don't use the flowers; use leaves only. However, there is discussion as to whether the flowers irritate at all.

Rattlesnake Master	*Eryngium yuccifolium, et al*	Asteraceae

Native, less common; found mostly north and east. Other species potentially may be used also.

 Root

 Late summer, early fall blooms

 Diuretic, secretory, analgesic

Tincture of dried root 1:5 60% (18)

Great xeriscape landscaping plant, low water and blooms well in heat

Annual wildflower with distinctive flower arrangements. The leaves of E. yuccifolium *are grasslike and the flowers are whitish, popcorn-type arrangements.*

Historical use of *E. yuccifolium* against bladder cancer and to treat pain and inflammation both internally and topically. Specific tribal use associated with respiratory and bladder complaints. Traditional use also against snakebites.

I have not used this yet, only grown it.

Red Root	*Ceanothus greggii, C. fendleri, C. herbaceus, C. americanus*	Rhamnaceae

Native; more common north and east in the state

 In some species only the root is used, and in others only the aboveground woody parts are used.

 In bloom in summer, harvest root in winter

 Astringent, lymphatic

Tincture 96% 1:2 root, some species aboveground woody parts fresh

Leaves used historically as New Jersey tea and have further use indicated by tribes of the Missouri River as a tea, as well as roots used for fuel. Roots are nitrogen fixers for soil. (144)

Perennial, deciduous to semievergreen shrub with small clusters of whitish flowers that get soapy when rubbed between fingers. Some species have a wintergreen scent to the leaves. Alternate leaves with whitish hairs on the underside.

Used to help in the digestion of fats and flush the lymph system, especially helpful with respiratory infections that are stuck. Used topically to help soothe inflammation and burns.

I have not harvested in Texas yet. I have gathered the aboveground parts in the Northwest US and the roots from the Arizona deserts.

Red Spiderling, Punarnava	*Boerhavia diffusa, B. coccinea, B. erecta, et al*	Nyctaginaceae

Native; found in Central Texas. *B. coccinea* is found in far west and far south Texas. Prefers full sun and heat.	
Aboveground parts	
Summer to early fall it is most vital, especially in droughts	
Tonic, analgesic, antimicrobial, antiviral, adaptogenic, immunomodulatory, hepatoprotective, diuretic	*Annual, clumping, low-growing, spreading, prostrate herb with reddish stems and tiny magenta flowers producing sticky fruits. Leaves are opposite and roundish.*
Not known. I have only tasted this fresh to get a sense of the effects.	
No other uses known.	

In Ayurveda this plant is most popularly used as a restorative tonic for all three *doshas*, or body types, and as a pain reliever. Herbalist Charlotte Jernigan totes it as being one of her most important allies in her practice of Ayurveda.

Popular Ayurvedic medicinal plant known as *punarnava*, the official species being *B. diffusa*. (145) (146)

Rhatany	*Krameria lanceolata*	Krameriaceae

Native; found in most of the state except for far east and coastal Texas

 Aboveground parts

 Spring

 Astringent

 Tincture fresh 1:2 96% or as a hot infusion

Vine, found as understory growth in fields with very small, needle-like, linear leaves and unique, striking, solitary, pink-to-magenta-colored flowers, rarely very abundant. Some species grow as grayish shrubs in Southwest deserts.

Root used as a dye by some tribes. (147)

Herbalist Michael Moore taught this as general astringent, mainly used as a gum wash. Its name actually means root for the teeth.

I have not had much experience with our native species in clinic and there are many other general astringents that can be used in its place.

Sage	*Salvia greggii, S. coccinea, S. farinacea, et al*	Lamiaceae

Many species native; more abundant throughout the central to western parts of the state		
Aboveground parts		
Spring and fall—may have several bloom periods depending on species		
Aromatic, astringent, dries up secretions		*Annual to perennial wildflower with varying colors of flowers depending on species, ranging from red to purple to pink. Leaves are opposite, simple, on a square stem, and vary in size by species. Many native sages can get woody and are mildly aromatic.*
I prefer native species in teas.		
Planted in xeriscapes and to attract pollinators		

Members of this genus are used to kill bacterial infections, especially in the respiratory tract. It helps to promote menstrual flow, dry up secretions, used when weaning children, as a topical disinfectant

Our wild sages are quite mild in aromatics compared to garden species and other states' wild sages like *S. apiana*. I do not use them much except in tea.

| Sagebrush, Mugwort | *Artemisia ludoviciana, A. campestris, et al* | Asteraceae |

Native and weedy; found in forested areas, open fields, and deserts. More central to north and western parts of the state.

 Leaves, aboveground non-woody parts

 Spring through summer

 Aromatic, bitter, antimicrobial, emmenagogic, antiparasitic

 As a tincture fresh 1:2 96%, drop dosage; vinegar 1:2 used topically for rashes. As a tea. Dried and burned in smudge sticks.

Some species are used as a visionary (entheogenic) herb, to smudge or clear the air, and to promote more intense dreams.

Perennial to annual herb with silvery-grayish, dissected leaves and very inconspicuous flowers along the top tips of the plant. The plant's leaves are soft to the touch and extremely aromatic, almost sweet. Most species are shrubbier and grow in the Southwest and the Panhandle. Some are more herbaceous and grow in Central Texas.

May be used to help encourage better digestive response in the body, stimulating to secretions, promotes menstruation, and kills germs topically

This genus includes notable plants like Mugwort and Wormwood. While there are variations by species, many native species are easy to propagate and great xeriscape plants. Do not confuse this with sage as is often done.

141

Native; more common in East Texas

 Leaves and bark

 Spring

 Alterative, demulcent

 Tea of leaves

Also used as a flavoring in root beer. The essential oil is used in perfumery.

Deciduous tree reaching about 15-20 feet with alternating, ovate leaves having 1-3 lobes. Male and female flowers on differing plants produce small, dark-purplish, egg-shaped fruits. Leaves smell a little citrusy when crushed.

Known as a spring tonic to help move blood. Leaves are tasty and soothing to mucous membranes. Herbalist and Permaculture Enthusiast Larry Ashley teaches that in East Texas folk use includes chewing twigs to help alleviate tobacco cravings.

Potential toxicity (concern over carcinogen) of the constituent safrole has led to a decline in use, and it was banned as a flavoring. Many modern herbalists continue to use it to this day.

Scrambled Eggs 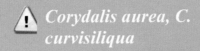 *Corydalis aurea, C. curvisiliqua*	Fumariaceae

Native, found in central, north and western part of the state	
Whole plant including root	
Early spring	
Analgesic, hypnotic	*Perennial to annual small wildflower. Found more prolifically with enough rain in late winter. Less than a foot tall with deeply dissected, compound leaves and topped with irregular yellow flowers. Entire plant is quite delicate and brief in its appearance.*
Tincture fresh 1:2 96%	
No other uses noted.	

Used in drop dosage to treat neural pain, shakiness, tremors, and as a sleep aid. Herbalist Ginger Webb uses the Texas species regularly in preparations.

CAUTION: *Very potent, use in drop dosage; some species are highly toxic.* There is a similar species popularly used in Chinese medicine.

Senna	*Cassia lindheimeri*	Fabaceae

Native and prolific around the Hill Country in Central Texas	
Leaves and pods	
Summer to Fall	
Cathartic laxative	*Shrubby perennial growing up to 5 feet tall with pinnately compound leaves and clusters of bright yellow flowers, forming pea-like pods. Leaves are soft, fuzzy, and stinky.*
None Noted	
Xeriscaping and wildscaping plant	

Well-known and widely used laxative. Not recommended.

CAUTION: *Using cathartic laxatives is not recommended.* Instead, try using something gentle like fiber first, rather than going straight to laxatives, which can also become addictive.

Shepherd's Purse	*Capsella bursa-pastoris*	Brassicaceae

Non-native and weedy; all over cities, especially in unmown yards, the cracks of sidewalks, and old agricultural fields	
Aboveground parts	
Winter to early spring	
Styptic, aromatic	*Annual herb topped with tiny clusters of white flowers producing heart-shaped seed pods that spiral down the stem. Grows up to 1 foot tall and forms dense stands.*
Fresh plant tincture 1:2 96%	
Used as a food in some Asian countries (148).	

Generally used in first aid situations to stop excessive bleeding. Can be used internally for postpartum hemorrhaging or topically on a bleeding wound.

Tincture will smell noticeably like gasoline. Nothing is wrong with your tincture, this is the smell of the plant.

Silk Tassel	*Garrya ovata*	Garryaceae

Native to the Hill Country and West Texas; seems to prefer some shade but needs little water

 Leaves

 Spring to summer

 Antispasmodic, seems to have affinity to gastrointestinal tract and uterus

 Fresh plant tincture 1:2 96%

Xeriscape and landscaping plant

Perennial evergreen shrub with simple, wavy, ovate leaves, somewhat tough and leathery, furry and white underneath. Flowers form dangling whitish tassels along branches in spring, which dry out to purple-black fruits.

Used to treat muscle spasms and pain, especially in the abdominal region

No special notes.

Skullcap	*Scutellaria drummondii, S. wrightii, S. ovata,*	Lamiaceae

Native; found all over Central, East, and North Texas. Some species are mostly in the Hill Country, especially as an understory in open fields or growing directly out of limestone rock.

 Aboveground parts in flower

 Spring

 Analgesic, bitter, sedative, hypnotic

 Fresh plant tincture 96% 1:2; as a glycerite 1:2 100%

No other uses noted.

Annual to perennial herb, field varieties are short, sparse, clumping and woody with small, rounded, opposite leaves, topped with blue-to-purple flowers that have a distinctive helmet shape, giving the plant its name. Some species may not be woody. Use flower to identify.

May be used to help reduce pain, calm down, and promote sleep. Especially helpful for headaches.

Field varieties are more bitter than the Hill Country *S. ovatum* species or commercially grown skullcap. The more bitter varieties may be more helpful for those with irritable bowels. Have not experimented yet with the landscaping variety that has pink flowers. Lookalike plants like *Teucrium spp* resemble skullcap and grow near it. Be careful to identify proper flower shape. Skullcap is a good alternative to kava. Expanded monograph available.

| Snakeroot, Birthwort |  *Aristolochia tomentosa, A. serpentaria, A. reticulata* | Aristolochiaceae |

Native and not very common; various species scattered through the west to the east, more towards the southern half of the state. Cultivate; do not gather wild.

 Whole plant, especially root

 Summer

 Alterative, immunomodulator

 Fresh plant tincture 1:2, root, 96% drop-dosage only

Folk use as reptile repellent. Strong smelling and attracts flies into it, trapping them into collecting pollen.

Perennial deciduous vine with simple, alternating leaves and a very unique, striking, flower in magenta to purple with somewhat inflated, tubular, united, colorful sepals thought to resemble a birth canal

Used in drop dosage as a strong tonic to wake up debilitated constitutions, especially after life-threatening situations (surgery, illness); traditional use during labor but due to toxicities it is discouraged for use in this way

TOXIC: *Proven to have a significant amount of carcinogenic activity in one of its constituents.* I have never found this plant in Texas. Snakeroot has an intimate relationship with the pipevine swallowtail caterpillar. This niche relationship makes it a no pick for herbalists, except in case of dire emergency or if you decide to propagate. I have not tried the Texas variety, but many species have been made into medicine. Not recommended for harvest (149).

Spicebush	*Lindera benzoin*	Lauraceae

Native; infrequent in Central Texas and far east in the swamps	
Leaves and fruit	
Spring through Summer	

Aromatic, alterative, diaphoretic, carminative, vermifuge	*Perennial, deciduous shrubby tree 6-12 feet tall. Leaves are obovate and alternate, dark green on top and light underneath, up to 6 inches long. Yellow flowers turn into glossy red berries. Aromatic and yummy-smelling!*
Infusion of leaves	
Very tasty; has a history of berries used as a culinary spice	

Used as a stimulating plant to help alleviate indigestion or help sweat out fevers

Have never found more than 1-2 trees at a time in Central Texas, so I only use this sparingly in practice. Spicebush swallowtail butterflies and certain moths pollinate it. Thanks to herbalist Ginger Webb for introducing me to this one.

Stork's Bill	*Erodium texanum*	Geraniaceae

Non-native and weedy; found in open fields and empty lots, most common in the central to the south of the state

 Whole plant

 Late winter to early spring and sometimes again in fall

 Astringent

 Tea

Annual, low-growing herb forming from a basal rosette, producing a few 5-petaled pink flowers clustered at the top, turning to beak-like seed pods, hence the name. Stems are sticky and hairy and leaves pinnate.

Can be used as a dye; also edible.

Used in Mexico especially, after birthing, to help tonify uterus and alleviate bleeding (150)

No special notes.

Sumac	*Rhus glabra, R. virens, R. trilobata, et al*	Anacardiaceae

Native; found Central to West Texas	
Leaves and berries	
Summer	
Astringent, refrigerant	*Perennial shrub creating red berries. Leaves vary by species, some pinnately compound, some simple. Shrub can get about 3 feet tall and dense.*
Leaves dried and powdered, berries in tea	
Landscaping	

Sour, sticky red berries used as a cooling tea. Herbalist Michael Moore taught that the leaves can be used dried and powdered to soothe chafed skin and to help tonify tissue.

TOXIC LOOKALIKE: *Make sure to identify properly.* Genus shared with *Rhus toxicodendron*, poison ivy, which causes contact dermatitis. Make sure to identify the proper plant. Poison ivy has trifoliate leaves and other distinguishing characteristics.

Sunflower	*Helianthus annuus, H. maximiliani, et al*	Asteraceae

Native, weedy; more prolific from the central through the western half of the state.

 Flowers, leaves, and seeds

 Summer to early fall

 Diuretic, expectorant

 Seeds and leaves as a tea (151)

Food, seeds for oil

Annual wildflower with showy, yellow, composite flowers and rough, hairy, sandpapery leaves growing up to 10 feet tall

The flowers and leaves of this plant are used to sooth inflammation and have a traditional use for respiratory complaints, coughs, etc.

The seed heads and leaves can be offered to chickens; they adore them! The dried stalks make a good fire starter. Please note that there are many, many plants in this family that look alike and may be misidentified for one another.

Sweet Clover	*Melilotus albus, et al*	Fabaceae

Non-native, weedy; found all over Texas in empty lots, fields, and old farms	
Aboveground parts dried	
Spring to fall intermittently	
Analgesic, emollient, astringent	*Annual herb with dark green, trifoliate leaves and topped with white flowers, some species yellow, growing up to 2 feet tall. Vanilla smell only upon wilting.*
Topically—dried into oil 1:5	
Perfumery, and was used to flavor vodka as a fake vanilla	

Remedy for pain associated with a sensation of coldness of the extremities and marked tenderness, also for pain associated with dysmenorrhea and other neuralgias

Presence of coumarins may be part of how this plant acts. (152)

Texas Paintbrush	*Castilleja indivisa*	Scrophulariaceae

Native; found all over fields and open sunny areas, especially in the eastern half of Texas	
All parts have a history of use	
Spring to summer	
Anti-inflammatory, emollient	*Annual to biennial wildflower with soft-looking, red-bracted spikes of flower arrangements growing about 1 foot tall*
Tea of flowers	
Some history of edibility and as a hair wash (153)	

Most history of use is from Native Tribes to affect the immune system and inflammation

This plant is a hemiparasite, which means it survives off some of the plants around it and can also concentrate selenium into it, so internal use is discouraged due to potential toxicities.

Tree of Heaven	*Ailanthus altissima*	Simaroubaceae

Non-native, weedy and invasive in most parts of the country; not as common in Texas, may be found in Central Texas

 Bark from small twigs

 Spring

 Antimicrobial, vermifuge, astringent, antianaphylactic, antimalarial

 Fresh plant tincture 1:2 96%; infusion of twigs

Was used as a landscaping tree until it became invasive. Some history of the wood used in furniture making.

Tall tree with pinnately compound leaves and male and female flowers on different trees. The female bears yellowish-green flowers producing flat, twisted, winged fruits. Grayish bark with owl head–like imprints, smells burnt or nutty.

The bark of this tree is used to treat diarrhea and amoebic and other parasitic infections, relax cardiac function, and assist in quelling asthmatic responses. Popular folk medicine in Asian countries.

Popular in traditional Chinese medicine, called *chun bai pi*. All parts are used in a variety of ways. Contains quassin, saponin, and ailanthone, which is antimalarial. There are too many compounds to list.

Trumpet Vine	*Campsis radicans*	Bignoniaceae

Native and weedy landscaping plant common in Central Texas. Quite enthusiastic and can take over sides of old buildings.

 Leaves and flowers

 Summer to fall

 Antifungal

 Tea of flowers

Landscaping vine

Perennial, deciduous, woody vine with extra large, showy, pendulous orange flowers and pinnately compound leaves with a large bean-like seed pod

May be effective to help kill fungal infections like Candidiasis in the body

Shares the same family as Desert Willow and Pau d'arco.

Vervain	*Verbena halei, V. canadensis, V. brasiliensis*	Verbenaceae

Native. *V. brasiliensis* is a non-native, invasive species, common in open fields and along roadsides. It's hard not to find an area in the state without a species. Extremely prolific genus, especially the *V. halei* species.

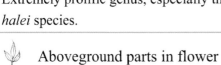 Aboveground parts in flower

 Spring, summer, and sometimes fall blooms; be sure to use while in bloom

 Bitter, aromatic, sedative, diaphoretic

Tincture fresh aboveground parts 1:2 96%

Annual to perennial, slender, erect wildflower with clusters of tiny purplish or pinkish flowers growing around top of the stem. Will reach between 8 inches to 5 feet depending on species.

Ancient stories regard this herb as sacred and used to ward off "evil" influences. Also used in Bach flower essence therapy.

I use this herb most often for hot, irritated, whiny folks, who are anxious and overwhelmed with life. Seems to be helpful in relaxing gut spasms and many irritable bowel syndrome sufferers have had success using it. Traditional use included helping the body to sweat out a fever, so it is often included in cold and flu formulas.

Expanded monograph available.

Violet	*Viola sororia, V. missouriensis, et al*	Violaceae

Native; found mostly in Central to East Texas

 Leaves and flowers

 Early Spring

 Demulcent, nutritive, vulnerary, diuretic

Perennial, herbaceous, evergreen, low-growing, clumping wildflower with simple heart-shaped leaves and purple-to-white, nodding, solitary flowers

 Infused oil made from dried parts; infusion or tea

Edible plant

Used internally to help soothe respiratory and digestive irritations. Externally, used to soothe inflammation and especially in breast oils to soften lumps.

Spreads easily in shade beds with mints.

Wafer Ash	*Ptelea trifoliata*	Rutaceae

Native; found more in a north-to-south belt along the center axis of the state

 Seeds and bark

 Spring

 Aromatic, bitter, antimicrobial, alterative

 Tincture of bark 1:2 96%; seeds as antimicrobial in tea or added to questionable water to help stop bacteria growth

Used as substitute for hops in beer making.

Small shrubby tree with trifoliate leaves. Clusters of yellowish flowers in early spring provide a delicious fragrance to hikers. Fruits dangle in clusters and look similar to ash, but the entire tree emits a citrusy scent.

Used somewhat like *Mahonia trifoliolata* (Agarita) to help stimulate digestion; also kills infections in the digestive tract

Contains some berberine like the plants in *Berberidaceae*. (154)

159

Walnut	*Juglans microcarpa, et al*	Juglandaceae

Native; found along waterways. Grows more in Central to West Texas.		
Leaves and hulls		
Spring to summer for leaves, fall for hulls and nuts		
Astringent, antiparasitic	*Medium-sized, deciduous tree with pinnately compound leaves and round fruits that turn from green to black. Looks very much like a pecan tree. Bark is in rough plates.*
Tincture of hulls 1:2 fresh 96%; leaves 1:2 96%	
Also used for dye and food. The nuts are thought to be good for the brain and fertility.	

Leaves used to help alleviate diarrhea. Herbalist Phyllis Light uses the hulls as a source of iodine for use in the treatment of hypothyroidism. In large doses, hulls have been used against parasites. (155)

The only visible differentiation between pecan and walnut is in the fruits, and the inner pith of the stems is chambered in walnut, or entire in pecans.

Wax Mallow	*Malvaviscus arboreus var. drummondii*	Malvaceae

Native; found in Central Texas, to the east and south, and into the Gulf Coast	
Whole plant and fruit	
Late summer and fall gives the biggest blooms, but it may bloom several times a year	
Demulcent	*Perennial shrub with simple, palmate leaves and topped with red, spiraling blooms. May form large and dense shrubs.*
Cold Infusion of flowers	
Fruits are edible in winter. Plant is used in xeriscaping and wildscaping.	

Soothes inflamed mucous membranes in the throat, stomach, and urinary tract

Root may be used for extra mucilage, but since you can get some slime out of the leaves and flowers, I leave the root alone. Also known commonly as Turk's Cap, a name I do not use, as I do not describe plants as looking like particular ethnic groups.

Wild Four O'clock	*Mirabilis texensis, M. latifolia, et al*	Nyctaginaceae

Native *M. texensis* is out west; *M. latifolia* is central		
Leaves and root		
Spring		
Anti-inflammatory, vulnerary, diuretic, purgative	*Herbaceous perennial wildflower. Texas varieties have small, deep-throated, pinkish-to-white flowers and opposite, sharp-pointed leaves.*	
None noted		
Some species are used for dye. (156)		

Used for weight loss and researched for its anti-inflammatory benefits

I have not used this plant.

Wild Cherry — *Prunus serotina* — Rosaceae

Native; found mostly in East Texas, isolated and scattered in the Hill Country

 Outer bark taken from small limbs and twigs

 Spring for bark

 Antispasmodic, expectorant

 Decocted into a reduced tea and made into a syrup

The edible fruits are used in jellies.

Tree with simple, oblong, serrated, shiny leaves; long clusters of white flowers turning into clusters of small, dark, drooping fruits. Mature trees with broken, dark gray-to-black bark.

Most popularly used in cough syrups to help sedate spastic coughing and make the coughing more productive

Potential toxicities are associated with this family. Berry pits and leaves contain cyanide in very small amounts, much like apples.

163

Wild Indigo	*Baptisia bracteata, B. australis, B. sphaerocarpa, et al*	Fabaceae

Native; especially to east and north Texas and into the Gulf Coast	
Leaves, bark, and sometimes root	
Summer	
Immunostimulant	*Small, perennial evergreen shrub with grayish-green, trifoliate leaves and pea-like, white flower growing about 2 feet tall.*
Tincture fresh root 1:2 96%	
Can also be used to make a blue dye. (157)	

Used during illness to help resolve infections, especially colds and flus that are hanging on. Historically used both topically and internally.

Thermopsis, a plant that grows in the higher elevations and may not be found in Texas, may be used similarly to *Baptisia*. This plant may be somewhat toxic so make sure to only harvest and use after proper guidance from an experienced wildcrafter or herbalist.

Wild Lettuce	*Lactuca serriola*	Asteraceae

Non-native, weedy and invasive; found more in the northern half of the state

 Aboveground parts

 Winter to early spring

 Nutritive, bitter, analgesic, calming

 Fresh aboveground parts in tincture 1:2 96%

The leaves are edible.

Annual herb. Large, basal rosettes producing central, reddish stem that extends upwards. Alternating, serrated, oblong leaves with a spine running along the underside of the midrib. Flowers are small, yellowish, and composite, clustering at the top. Sap is white latex.

Used to treat headaches, help promote sleep, and encourage better milk production in nursing mothers

Can be confused with several plants that look similar: dandelion, sow thistle, and Texas dandelion. Make sure you identify it properly.

Non-native, weedy; found all over open fields more in the central to southern parts of the state, from west to east, even on the coast

 Leaves, stems, milky seeds

 Spring

 Trophorestorative to nervous system, calming, nutritive

Annual grass with clusters of pendulous, dangling seed heads. When ripe and ready for harvest, seeds squirt a white latex when squeezed.

Milky seed fresh in 50% 1:2. Leaves dried,cut up, and decocted—yum! Thanks to Herbalist and Mentor Margi Flint for that preparation.

Edible, cultivated and used as food

Oats are used as a nutritive tonic to help soothe and restore the nervous system to balance. (158) They are high in calcium, potassium, magnesium, and B vitamins. (159)

Expanded monograph available.

Wild Onion	*Allium canadense, et al*	Liliaceae

Native; found mostly from the center throughout the eastern half of the state.

 Whole plant

 Winter to early spring

 Stimulant, antimicrobial, anti-inflammatory, anthelmintic, expectorant, antispasmodic, tonic, drawing

Perennial herb with dense clumps of linear leaves and clusters of white-to-pink flowers, making small bulblets, which have a strong onion scent when crushed

Fresh topical poultice—mash whole plant to draw infection, chest colds, alleviate coughing. Add chopped leaves to meals.

Edible as a culinary spice

All parts can be mashed and put on an area of the skin to draw out infection, inflammations, and chest colds

TOXIC LOOKALIKE: Crow poison comes out around the same time but has no smell. Make sure you properly identify this plant.

Willow	*Salix spp*	Salicaceae

Native; found in most parts of the state		
Outer bark peeled from small limbs		
Summer		
Analgesic, bitter, sedative, anti-inflammatory	*Deciduous tree with multiple linear leaves and long catkins of yellowish flowers, turning into puff-like seeds.*	
Fresh outer bark 1:2 96%		
Rooting hormone in branches used by gardeners		

Contains salicylates and is used to help bring down fevers, topically and internally to help relieve pain and inflammation.

Used very similarly to cottonwood, its cousin. According to herbalist Michael Moore, cottonwood is slightly more stable in its constituents.

Wind Flower ⚠ *Anemone berlandieri, et al*	Ranunculaceae

Native; found throughout the Rio Grande Valley up into central, somewhat north, and east Texas	
Aboveground parts in flower	

Winter to early spring	
Calming and hypotensive. Drop dosage use only.	*Perennial wildflower with trifoliate leaves found near the flower stem but not connected. The flower stem is topped with a solitary flower ranging from white to pink to purplish. Some species may have two flowers. The flowers are subtended by bracts, leaf like structures.*
Fresh plant tincture 1:10 96%. DROP DOSAGE: 3-5 drops.	
No other uses noted.	

Used by experienced herbalists for dry, chilly, deficient, depressive states. A plant for people dealing with fear issues, despair, exhaustion, PMS, frontal headaches, low blood sugar, adrenaline kicks, shakiness, unresolved sexual baggage, and panic attacks. Diminishes cerebral spinal fluid in head and sends everything down. Can cause loss of consciousness and dangerously lower blood pressure.

TOXIC: *Not recommended.* Many species are used medicinally, but the effect ranges from toxic to extremely toxic. Caustic to touch; use care if you ever harvest. Dry plant inert. The fresh plant tincture does not have long shelf life. Wind flower can create a very strong effect when taken and lowers blood pressure, almost dangerously, especially if more than a few drops are used. Use is discouraged due to the constituent protoanemonin.

GLOSSARY OF TERMS

Please note: any and all botanical terms we missed that you may not recognize can be found in most Texas field guides, which you should definitely form large collections of if this is your passion!

Abortifacient: May influence or cause abortion

Adaptogenic: Nondirectional, amphoteric action, as in a herb that seems to have a normalizing effect on the body and helps it to adapt better to stresses

Alterative: An action of restoring the body back to health by helping with the function of eliminative channels. Historically, these herbal agents would have also been called blood purifiers.

Analgesic: Relieves pain

Annual: A plant that dies at the end of one year.

Anthelmintic: Prefer the term vermifuge; an agent that expels or kills parasites

Antihistamine: An agent that inhibits the release of histamine, a compound released during allergic episodes

Antioxidant: A substance that inhibits damaging oxidation and retards the breakdown of healthy, living cells

Antioxidative: See antioxidant

Antispasmodic: Agent that relieves spasm in muscles

Astringent: Agent that causes the contraction of body tissues, most often used on skin to prevent bleeding and treat inflammation

Biennial: A plant that lives for two years, and reproduces in the second year.

Bioremediator: Microorganisms that are introduced to an area to help break down toxic substances or environmental pollutants

Cardioprotective: Protective to the heart and cardiovascular system

Cardiotonic: Tonifying to the heart

Carminative: Relieving flatulence and gas

Chemopreventative: Agent used to prevent cancer

Cholesterolgenic: Containing cholesterol

Counterirritant: An agent that heats or irritates the skin to counteract underlying pain or discomfort

Cyanogenic: Containing cyanide

Decoction: Simmering plant material in water for at least 20 minutes.

Deciduous: As in a tree or shrub, which loses its vegetation or leaves, annually

Demulcent: Relieving inflammation or irritation with a protective film caused by mucilaginous components

Diaphoretic: Inducing perspiration

Diuretic: Increasing the flow of urine

Emetic: Causing vomiting

Emmenagogic: Stimulating blood flow in the pelvic region and uterus and may cause menstruation

Emollient: Having or possessing the quality of softening or soothing the skin

Endemic: A plant restricted in native range to a very specialized area

Entheogen: A plant substance ingested to produce an altered or different state of consciousness, usually used for religious or spiritual purposes.

Expectorant: A substance that promotes or facilitates the secretion of phlegm or mucus from the respiratory tract

Evergreen: A plant that has green leaves throughout the year.

Galactagogue: Increasing or promoting breast milk production

Glycerite: Extract made in a base of glycerin. Appropriate amount of plant material is soaked for a time in appropriate amount of glycerin and then strained. Generally plant material is macerated.

Hemiparasite: A plant that may obtain part of its nutrition through parasitizing

Hepatoprotective: Preventing damage or protective to the liver

Hydroscopic: The ability to attract and hold water molecules

Hypertensive: Exhibiting high blood pressure

Hypoglycemic: Abnormally low level of glucose in the blood

Hypotensive: Low blood pressure

Immunomodulatory: A substance that affects the functioning of the immune system

Infusion: Soaking plant material in wither hot or cold water for at least 20 minutes if hot, several hours if cold.

172

Insuloregulating: Invented term to describe a substance that balances or stabilizes blood sugar

Latex: Milky fluid in plants consisting of proteins, starches and alkaloids, sugars, oils, tannins, resins and/or gums present in about 10% of plants, different from synthetic latex

Nutritive: Providing nourishment through micronutrients (minerals, protein, essential fatty acids)

Obovate: Ovate shape, narrower at base

Palmate: Leaf shaped like a hand

Perennial: A plant that lives for more than two years, generally through underground food storage mechanisms, usually woody

Pinnate: Compound leaf arranged or shaped like a feather

Refrigerant: Cooling

Rhizomes: Underground lateral stems that may shoot rootlets off to help spread a colony of plants

Rubefacient: A substance that when applied to the skin will produce redness by dilating capillaries and causing blood flow to an area

Scorpioid: A flower arrangement that unfurls flowers like a scorpion its tail, uncurling as the flowers develop

Secretory: Related to or promoting secretions to be created

Sedative: Sedating, producing calmness or promoting sleep

Stimulant: Raising levels of physiologic or nervous activity

Stomachic: Promoting appetite or assisting with digestion

Sympathomimetic: An agent that mimics the fight or flight response in the nervous system

Tincture: Extract of plant made by soaking the appropriate amount of plant material in the appropriate amount of grain or other food grade alcohol for a length of time, then straining and saving the remaining liquid. Generally plant material is macerated.

Trifoliate: Compound leaf with three leaflets

Vermifuge: Term also used for anthelmintic

Vulnerary: An agent used to help heal wounds

Xeriscape: Landscaping that requires little or no irrigation, usually by using drought tolerant plants and/or plants adapted to an area

ADDITIONAL RESOURCES

Other Publications Available from Author Nicole Telkes

- *Wildflower School Medicinal Plant Allies Workbook: Expanded Monographs on Central Texas Plants*
- *Medicinal Plants of Texas Photobook*

For a full list of books, websites, resources for obtaining seeds and plants, and a more extensive list of botanicals you can go to **www.nicoletelkes.com** and click on the medicinal plant information link.

Check the Wildflower School of Botanical Medicine's website, www.wildflowerherbschool.com for a full list of educational links we update, as well as blogs on Texas plants, and Medicinal Plants of Texas, http://weedcrafter.blogspot.com/.

Resources

- Texas native plants to grow at home are available twice a year from the Lady Bird Johnson Wildflower Center during their plant sales (and you can buy my Wildflower tea there). https://www.wildflower.org/

- Native Plant Society of Texas has good information on natives and a great email list where you can ID out plants. www.npsot.org

- Martin Simonton of New World Botanicals has really great, hard to find native Texas medicinal plants from East Texas. His Facebook page is
  https://www.facebook.com/newworldbotanical

- Marjory Wildcraft is an excellent resource to learn how to grow things using permaculture concepts, especially in Texas. http://growyourowngroceries.org/

- Michael Eason created a great site for identifying Texas plants. http://txflora.org/

- Visit Texas Master Naturalist Program to learn more about your region. http://txmn.org/

- Texas Master Gardener Program. http://mastergardener.tamu.edu/

Books

- Delana Tull has a great book *Edible and Useful Plants of Texas and the Southwest: A Practical Guide Paperback* – January 1, 1999. I also enjoy her field guide, *Field Guide to Wildflowers, Trees and Shrubs of Texas*. It has good keys.

- *The Useful Wild Plants of Texas* with Scooter Cheatham and Lynn Marshall offers extensive Encyclopedias on everything you could possibly want to know about Texas plants.

- *Wildflowers of the Texas Hill Country* by Marshall Enquist is a great field guide.

- *Wildflowers of the Western Plains: A Field Guide*, Paperback – September 1, 2008 by Zoe Merriman Kirkpatrick is a great resource for Central to West Texas and the Panhandle.

- *Medicinal Plants of the Desert and Canyon West: A Guide to Identifying, Preparing, and Using Traditional Medicinal Plants Found in the Deserts and Canyons of the West and Southwest* by Michael Moore is a helpful resource for West Texas deserts.

- *Edible Plants of the Gulf South*, paperback by Charles Allen and Harry Winters is a great resource for East Texas.

- *Native and Naturalized Woody Plants of Austin and the Hill Country* by Daniel Lynch

- *Trees, Shrubs, and Woody Vines of the Southwest: A Guide for the States of Arkansas, Louisiana, New Mexico, Oklahoma and Texas*, Hardcover – January 1, 1960 by Robert A. Vines.

A note on the references. Some of the information included in this book, is commonly held by herbal clinicians. All uses and information not cited are due to them being folk, or common information from traditional or clinical experience. Much of this common knowledge comes from physiomedicalist, and eclectic physicians as well as mystics and folk healers.

REFERENCES

1. **Leal, Ana.** Agave (Agave spp.) and its Traditional Products as a Source of Bioactive Compounds. *Academia.ediu.* [Online] Bentham Science Publishers, 2012.
http://www.academia.edu/4471620/Agave_Agave_spp._and_its_Traditional_Products_as_a_Source_of_Bioactive_Compounds.

2. **L.** Agave americana. *Plants For A Future.* [Online]
http://www.pfaf.org/user/Plant.aspx?LatinName=Agave+americana.

3. **Kress, Henriette.** Amaranthus. *Henriette's Herbal.* [Online]
http://www.henriettesherbal.com/eclectic/rafinesque/amaranthus.html.

4. **KINGHORN, WILLIAM P. JONES and A. DOUGLAS.** PubMedCentral:BIOLOGICALLY ACTIVE NATURAL PRODUCTS OF THE GENUS CALLICARPA. *U.S. National Library of Medicine.* [Online] June 1, 2008.
http://www.ncbi.nlm.nih.gov/pmc/articles/PMC2760847/.

5. **Duke, James.** Apios americana Medik. *Purdue University Center for new Crops and Plants Products.* [Online] 1983.
http://www.hort.purdue.edu/newcrop/duke_energy/Apios_americana.html#Folk Medicine.

6. **Moore, Michael.** Abstracts: Rudbeckia. *Southwest School of Botanical Medicine .* [Online]
http://wolf.mind.net/swsbm/Abstracts/Rudbeckia-AB.txt.

7. **Duerr, Sasha.** *The Handbook of Natural Plant Dyes: Personalize Your Craft with Organic Colors from Acorns, Blackberries, Coffee, and Other Everyday Ingredients.* Portland : Timber Press, 2010.

8. **Deane, Green.** Valuable Viburnums. *Eat the Weeds and Other Things Too.* [Online] http://www.eattheweeds.com/valuable-viburnums/.

9. **Georgina Robinson, George Agurkis, Anthony Scerbo.** Medical Attributes of Eupatorium perfoliatum - Boneset. *Biology Department*

Wilkes University. [Online] July 2007.
http://klemow.wilkes.edu/Eupatorium.html.

10. **L.** Eupatorium perfoliatum - L. *Plants for a Future.* [Online]
http://www.pfaf.org/user/Plant.aspx?LatinName=Eupatorium+perfoliatu
m.

11. **Bergner, Sasha Daucus and Paul.** Eupatorium: Clinical
correspondence and commentary. *Medical Herbalism: Journal for the
CLinical Practitioner.* [Online] 1 31, 1996.
http://medherb.com/Materia_Medica/Eupatorium_-
_Clinical_Correspondence_and_commentary.htm.

12. **Carlo Calabrese, N.D., et al.** Effects of a Standardized Bacopa
monnieri Extract on Cognitive Performance, Anxiety, and Depression in
the Elderly............ [Online] July 2008.
http://www.ncbi.nlm.nih.gov/pmc/articles/PMC3153866/.

13. **Sunil Dutt Shukla1, 2, Maheep Bhatnagar2 and Sukant
Khurana.** Critical evaluation of ayurvedic plants for stimulating intrinsic
antioxidant response. *Frontiers in Neuroscience.* [Online] July 26, 2012.
http://journal.frontiersin.org/Journal/10.3389/fnins.2012.00112/full.

14. **Goswami S, Saoji A, Kumar N, Thawani V, Tiwari M, Thawani
M.** Effect of Bacopa monnieri on Cognitive functions in Alzheimer's .
IJCRIMPH. [Online] 2011.
http://www.iomcworld.com/ijcrimph/files/v03-n04-01.pdf.

15. **A Navarrete, F Palacios-Espinosa , R Mata.** Gastroprotective
Effect of Brickellia cavanillesii (Cav) B. L. Robinson (Asteraceae)....
Planta Medica. 2011, 77.

16. **Karl-Heinz A. Rosler, Robert S. Goodwin , Tom J. Mabry ,
Shambhu D. Varma , John Norris.** Flavonoids with Anti-Cataract
Activity from Brickellia arguta. *Journal of Natural Products.* 1984, Vol.
2, 47.

17. **Identification of Bioactive Agents from Plants. *National Center
for Pharmaceutical Crops (NCPC).* [Online] Arthur Temple College**

of Forestry and Agriculture, 2010. Arthur Temple College of Forestry and Agriculture.

18. Moore, Michael. *Personal Communication, The Southwest School of Botanical Medicine.* 2001.

19. Kane, Charles. *Herbal Medicine of the American Southwest.* Tucson : Lincoln Town Press, 2006.

20. Susan Belsinger, Deni Bown, Dr. James A. "Jim" Duke, Ph.D., Gayle Engels et al. Calendula Guide. *Herb Society of America.* [Online] http://www.herbsociety.org/factsheets/Calendula%20Guide.pdf.

21. Gené RM1, Segura L, Adzet T, Marin E, Iglesias J. Heterotheca inuloides: anti-inflammatory and analgesic effect. *PubMed.Gov.* [Online] March 1998. http://www.ncbi.nlm.nih.gov/pubmed/9582006.

22. Coballase-Urrutia E1, Pedraza-Chaverri J, Camacho-Carranza R, Cárdenas-Rodríguez N, et al. Antioxidant activity of Heterotheca inuloides extracts and of some of its metabolites. *PubMed.gov.* [Online] Sept 20, 2010. http://www.ncbi.nlm.nih.gov/pubmed/20620188.

23. Turner, Matt Warnock. *Remarkable Plants of Texas: Uncommon Accounts of Our Common Natives.* Austin : UT Press, 2009.

24. Caldecott, Todd. Lobelia. *Learning Herbs.* [Online] http://www.toddcaldecott.com/index.php/herbs/learning-herbs/305-lobelia.

25. Lloyd. Gelsemium. *Southwest School of Botanical Medicine.* [Online] http://www.swsbm.com/ManualsOther/Gelsemium-Lloyd.PDF.

26. [Online] http://botanical.com/botanical/mgmh/g/gelsem07.html.

27. King. Gelsemium: Kings. *Henrietta's Herbal.* [Online] http://www.henriettesherbal.com/eclectic/kings/gelsemium.html.

28. Vosnaki, Elena. Perfumery Material: Cassie & Mimosa & Differences with Cassia & Cassis. *Perfume Shrine.* [Online] May 23, 2012. http://perfumeshrine.blogspot.com/2012/05/perfumery-material-cassie-mimosa.html.

29. Gardea-Torresdey, J.L., et al. Adsorption of Toxic Metal Ions from Solution by Inactivated Cells of Larrea tridentata (Creosote Bush). *The Great Plains/Rocky Mountain Hazardous Substance Research Center.* [Online] April 2, 2001. http://www.engg.ksu.edu/HSRC/JHSR/v1_no3.html.

30. Webb, R. H., Fenstermaker, L., Heaton, J., & Hughson, D. *The Mojave Desert: Ecosystem Processes and Sustainability.* Reno : University of Nevada Press, 2009.

31. *Creosote Bush: Long-Lived Clones In The Mojave Desert.* Vasek, F. C. 67, American Journal of Botany, pp. 246-255.

32. Reyes-López, M., Villa-Treviño, S., Arriaga-Alba, M., Alemán-Lazarini, L., Rodríguez-Mendiola, M., Arias-Castro, C., et al. The amoebicidal aqueous extract from Castela texana possesses antigenotoxic and antimutagenic properties. *National Center for Biotechnology Information.* [Online] February 2005. http://www.ncbi.nlm.nih.gov/pubmed/15582360.

33. Facciola, S. *Cornucopia: A Source Book of Edible Plants.* Vista : Kampong Publications, 1990.

34. Kinsey, T. Beth. Malva parviflora – Cheeseweed Mallow. *Southeastern Arizon Wildflowers and the Plants of the Sonoran Desert.* [Online] http://www.fireflyforest.com/flowers/1479/malva-parviflora-cheeseweed-mallow/.

35. Plants of Texas Rangelands: Chinaberry. *Texas A&M AgriLife Extension Service.* [Online] http://essmextension.tamu.edu/plants/plant/chinaberry/.

36. Kress, Henriette. Cleavers coffee. *Henriette's Herbal.* [Online] August 2, 1995.

http://www.henriettesherbal.com/archives/best/1995/cleavercoffee.html.

37. Miller, George Oxford. *Landscaping with Native Plants of the Southwest.*

38. [Online] http://www.arkat-usa.org/get-file/19602/.

39. [Online] http://www.medicinatradicionalmexicana.unam.mx/monografia.php?l=3&t=&id=7017.

40. [Online] http://www.sciencedirect.com/science/article/pii/S0367326X06000839.

41. [Online] http://onlinelibrary.wiley.com/doi/10.1002/ptr.1161/abstract.

42. [Online] http://radicalbotany.com/2012/12/11/black-cottonwood-and-the-balm-of-gilead-populus-balsamifer-ssp-trichocarpa/.

43. [Online] http://www.eattheweeds.com/erodium-circutarium-geranium-carolinianum-two-bills-you-want-to-get-2/.

44. [Online] http://www.wildflower.org/plants/result.php?id_plant=GECA5.

45. Wild Geranium with Jim McDonald. *Pinterest.* [Online] Herb TV, 2013. http://www.pinterest.com/pin/352054895841333028/.

46. [Online] http://www.pfaf.org/user/Plant.aspx?LatinName=Lagerstroemia+indica.

47. Anderson, Neil O. *Flower Breeding and Genetics: Issues, Challenges and Opportunities for the 21st Century* .

48. [Online] http://www.sciencedirect.com/science/article/pii/S0378874103001223.

49. [Online]
http://www.lassens.com/ns/DisplayMonograph.asp?StoreID=v92hgb
d7x6sr2lr60g03n0et9mr4bdf3&DocID=bottomline-banaba.

50. Wood, Matthew. *The Earthwise Herbal: A Complete Guide to New World Medicinal Plants.*

51. Johnson, Laurence. *A Manual of the Medical Botany of North America.*

52. Grieve, Mrs M. Cucmber Pellitory. *A Modern Herbal.* [Online]
http://botanical.com/botanical/mgmh/p/pelwal22.html.

53. [Online]
http://www.pfaf.org/user/Plant.aspx?LatinName=Parietaria+officina
lis.

54. Moerman, D. E. *Native American Ethnobotany.* Portland :
Timber Press, 1998.

55. [Online] http://medplant.nmsu.edu/chilopsis.shtm.

56. [Online]
http://www.aridzonetrees.com/AZT%20Guest%20Articles/Desert%
20Willow_Not%20Just%20Another%20Pretty%20Face.htm.

57. [Online] http://www.henriettesherbal.com/eclectic/kings/aralia-spin.html.

58. [Online]
http://www.pfaf.org/user/Plant.aspx?LatinName=Aralia+spinosa.

59. Strobel, B. B. *An Experimental Enquiry Into the Medical Properties of the Aralia Spinosa ...*

60. Coxe, John Redman. *The American Dispensatory, Containing the Natural, Chemical, Pharmaceutical ...*

61. [Online] http://botanical.com/botanical/mgmh/b/bitroo47.html.

62. [Online] http://en.wikipedia.org/wiki/Apocynum_cannabinum.

63. [Online] http://www.henriettesherbal.com/eclectic/ellingwood/apocynum-cann.html.

64. [Online] http://en.uuuwell.com/mytag.php?id=21982.

65. [Online] http://www.sacredearth.com/ethnobotany/plantprofiles/elder.php.

66. Grieve, Margaret. *A Modern Herbal (Volume 1, A-H): The Medicinal, Culinary, Cosmetic and Economic Properties, Cultivation and Folk-Lore of Herbs, Grasses, Fungi, Shrubs & Trees with Their Modern Scientific Uses.* s.l. : Dover Publications, 1971.

67. [Online] http://www.hort.purdue.edu/newcrop/ncnu07/pdfs/charlebois284-292.pdf.

68. [Online] http://en.wikipedia.org/wiki/Elm#Wood.

69. [Online] http://scholarcommons.usf.edu/cgi/viewcontent.cgi?article=2664&context=etd.

70. Chrisp. Species At-Risk. *United Plant Savers.* [Online] May 8, 2012. http://www.unitedplantsavers.org/content.php/121-species-at-risk.

71. [Online] http://medicinewomansroots.blogspot.com/2007/05/fogotten-tonic-herb-evening-primrose.html.

72. [Online] http://www.henriettesherbal.com/eclectic/cook/ONOSMODIUM_VIRGINIANUM.htm.

73. Cook, William Henry. *The Physio-medical Dispensatory: A Treatise on Therapeutics, Materia Medica, and Pharmacy, in Accordance with the Principles of Physiological Medication.* 1869.

74. Boericke, William. Homeopathic Materia Medica. *Homéopathe International.* [Online] Médi-T, 2000. http://www.homeoint.org/books/boericmm/.

75. [Online] http://www.ncbi.nlm.nih.gov/pubmed/21571029.

76. R., Buchanan. *A Weavers Garden.*

77. [Online] http://www.ncbi.nlm.nih.gov/pubmed/9781305.

78. [Online] http://libproject.hkbu.edu.hk/was40/detail?channelid=1288&lang=en&record=81.

79. Brounstein, Howie. *Personal Communication, Columbines School of Botanical Studies.* 2001.

80. [Online] http://www.ncbi.nlm.nih.gov/books/NBK92770/.

81. [Online] http://pubs.acs.org/subscribe/journals/mdd/v05/i04/html/04news4.html.

82. [Online] http://onlinelibrary.wiley.com/doi/10.1002/mnfr.200700072/abstract;jsessionid=0538D9B9D27AC9686E547614FD31968F.d01t01.

83. [Online] http://www.burnsjournal.com/article/S0305-4179(01)00039-0/abstract.

84. Scott, Timothy L. *Invasive Plant Medicine: The Ecological Benefits and Healing Abilities of Invasives.* Rochester : Healing Arts Press, 2010.

85. Heaton, E., Voigt, T., and Long, S. P. A quantitative review comparing the yields of two candidate C4 perennial biomass crops in relation to nitrogen, temperature and water. *Biomass and Bioenergy.* 2004, 27, pp. 21-30.

86. Perdue, R. E. Arundo donax – Source of Musical Reeds and Industrial Cellulose. *Economic Botany.* 1958, 12, pp. 368-404.

87. Mirza, N., Mahmood, Q., Pervez, A., Ahmad, R., Farooq, R., Shah, M.M., Azim, M.R. Phytoremediation potential of Arundo donax in arsenic-contaminated synthetic wastewater. *Bioresource Technology.* 2010, 101, pp. 5815-9.

88. [Online] http://www.aseanbiodiversity.info/Abstract/51006851.pdf.

89. [Online] http://www.sciencedirect.com/science/article/pii/S0378874104006336.

90. [Online] http://www.ncbi.nlm.nih.gov/pmc/articles/PMC3228589/.

91. Hogan, Personal communication with herbalists Michael Moore and Phyllis.

92. [Online] http://www.mtnativeplants.org/filelib/41.pdf.

93. [Online] http://content.time.com/time/magazine/article/0,9171,881890,00.html .

94. [Online] http://www.hort.purdue.edu/newcrop/duke_energy/Vitis_vinifera.ht ml.

95. Robin Rose Bennett, Herbalist.

96. [Online] http://www.eattheweeds.com/smilax-a-brier-and-that%E2%80%99s-no-bull/.

97. Zavaleta, Antonio Noe Ph D. *Medicinal Plants of the Borderlands: A Bilingual Resource Guide* .

98. Grieve, Mrs M. *A Modern Herbal.*

99. [Online] http://extension.oregonstate.edu/bridges/osu-studies-homegrown-sources-fuel-rubber-and-fiber.

100. [Online] http://www.alandiashram.org/gurukula_blog/2012/03/grindelia-squarrosa-an-ayurvedic-view.html.

101. Yalcin, Funda N., Kaya, D. Ethnobotany, Pharmacology and Phytochemistry of the Genus Lamium (Lamiaceae). *Fabad Journal of Pharmaceutical Sciences.* 2006, Vol. 31, 1, pp. 43-52.

102. Nugroho, A., Choi, Jun-Kil, et al. Two New Flavonol Glycosides from Lamium amplexicaule L. and Their in vitro Free Radical Scavenging and Tyrosinase Inhibitory Activities. *Wordpress.* [Online] Planta Medica, 2009. http://agn19.files.wordpress.com/2011/06/pm-2009-364-printed-edition1.pdf.

103. [Online] http://www.wildflower.org/expert/show.php?id=4446&frontpage=true.

104. [Online] ttp://practicalplants.org/wiki/Basketry.

105. [Online] https://www.planetherbs.com/michaels-blog/honeysuckle-taking-the-bitter-with-the-sweet.html.

106. [Online] http://www.onlyfoods.net/marrubium-vulgare.html.

107. [Online] http://www.highlandsnd.com/botanical_materia_medica/Marrubium vulgare.htm.

108. [Online] http://www.herbaltransitions.com/materiamedica/Equisetum.htm.

109. Katz, Sandor. *Wild Fermentation: The Flavor, Nutrition, and Craft of Live-Culture Foods.* s.l. : Chelsea Green Publishing, 2003.

110. Mueller, W.F., Bedell, G.W., Shojaee, S., Jackson, P.J. Bioremediation of TNT Wastes by Higher Plants. *Proceedings of the 10th Annual Conference on Hazardous Waste Research.* [Online] April 2, 2001. http://www.engg.ksu.edu/HSRC/95Proceed/mueller.pdf.

111. Pasternakiewicz, Anna. Detoxification of Environmental Pollutants. [Online] September 12, 2013. http://www.environment.lviv.ua/fileadmin/user_upload/workshops_1 A/5.%201A%20Detox%20of%20environm%20pollutants%20A.%2 0Pasternakiewicz.pdf.

112. C Rivas-Morales, MA Oranday-Cardenas, MJ Verde-Star, ME Morales Rubio, EJ Mier Ortiz, E Garza-Gonzalez. Activity of extracts from two Eysenhardtia species against microorganisms related to urinary tract infections. *British Journal of Biomedical Science.* [Online] 2009. http://scholar.google.com/citations?view_op=view_citation&hl=bg& user=sBaEJAEAAAAJ&citation_for_view=sBaEJAEAAAAJ:zYLM 7Y9cAGgC.

113. [Online] http://www.texasbeyondhistory.net/st-plains/nature/images/chenopod.html.

114. *A Review on Medicinal Properties of Lantana camara.* Kalita, Sanjeeb, Gaurav Kumar, Loganathan Karthik, Kokati Venkata Bhaskara Rao. Tamil, Nadu India : VIT University.

115. Honeychurch, Penelope N. *Caribbean Wild Plants and Their Uses: An Illustrated Guide to Some Medicinal and Wild Ornamental Plants of the West Indies .*

116. Lantana. *Veterinary Medicine Library.* [Online] University of Illinois at Urbana-Champaign Library. http://www.library.illinois.edu/vex/toxic/lantana/lantana.htm#toxic.

117. *Jatropha bio-diesel production and use.* Achten W.M.J., Verchot L., Franken Y.J., Mathijs E., Singh V.P., Aerts R., Muys B. 12, s.l. : Biomass and Bioenergy, 2008, Vol. 32, pp. 1063-1084.

118. [Online] http://www.hort.purdue.edu/newcrop/morton/loquat.html.

119. [Online] https://www.planetherbs.com/specific-herbs/loquat-leaf-fruit-and-seed.html.

120. [Online] http://www.carvoeiro.com/history/medronho.

121. [Online] http://www.herbworld.com/learningherbs/MAGNOLIa%20_ho%20 po_.pdf.

122. Afifi, F.U. Hypoglycemic Effects of Prosopis fracta. *informa Healthcare.* [Online] Department of Pharmacognosy Faculty of Pharmacy, University of Jordan, 1993. http://informahealthcare.com/doi/abs/10.3109/13880209309082933?j ournalCode=phb.

123. [Online] http://www.henriettes- herb.com/eclectic/kings/polygala.html.

124. [Online] Wong, Ming (1976). La Médecine chinoise par les plantes. Le Corps a Vivre series. Éditions Tchou..

125. [Online] http://sylvanbotanical.com/2010/07/26/calming-the- spirit-with-albizia/.

126. [Online] http://www.yinyanghouse.com/theory/herbalmedicine/bo_he_tcm_he rbal_database.

127. [Online] http://kaleidoscope.cultural- china.com/en/7Kaleidoscope5334.html.

128. [Online] http://doctorschar.com/archives/siberian-motherwort- leonorus-sibiricus/.

129. [Online] http://www.susunweed.com/Article_Motherwort.htm.

130. [Online] http://www.intechopen.com/books/glucose- tolerance/medicinal-plants-and-natural-compounds-from-the-genus- morus-moraceae-with-hypoglycemic-activity-a-re.

131. [Online] http://www.hort.purdue.edu/newcrop/duke_energy/morus_alba.html .

132. [Online] http://www.fspublishers.org/published_papers/70394_..pdf.

133. *A Barefoot Doctors Manual. Running Press ISBN 0-914294-92-X.*

134. [Online] http://www.ncbi.nlm.nih.gov/pmc/articles/PMC2677726/.

135. [Online] E. Viveros-Va, C. Rivas-Mora, A. Oranday-Ca, M.J. Verde-Star, P. Carranza-Ra: Antimicrobial Activity of Hedeoma drummondii against Opportunistic Pathogens. Pakistan Journal of Biological Sciences. Apr 2011, Vol. 14, No. 4: 305-307.

136. [Online] http://www.hindawi.com/journals/ecam/2012/596524/ http://onlinelibrary.wiley.com/doi/10.1002/ptr.1210/abstract .

137. [Online] http://www.life-enhancement.com/magazine/article/193-almost-everything-you-want-to-know-about-vinpocetine.

138. Grieve, M. Periwinkles. *Botanical.com.* [Online] http://botanical.com/botanical/mgmh/p/periwi27.html.

139. Tull, Delana. *Edible and Medicinal Plants of Texas and the Southwest.*

140. [Online] http://herbs-treatandtaste.blogspot.com/2011/01/vervain-verbena-officinalis-healing.html.

141. [Online] http://www.texasbeyondhistory.net/ethnobot/images/prickly-poppy.html.

142. [Online] http://www.nutrition-and-you.com/purslane.htm.

143. [Online] http://www.texasbeyondhistory.net/ethnobot/images/purslane.html.

144. New Jersey Tea. *United States Department of Agriculture, Natural Resources Conservation Service.* [Online] August 15, 2011. https://plants.usda.gov/factsheet/pdf/fs_ceam.pdf.

145. [Online] http://www.isca.in/IJPS/Archive/v1i1/6.ISCA-RJPcS-2012-001.pdf.

146. [Online] http://examine.com/supplements/Boerhaavia+Diffusa/.

147. Rhatany. *Herbal Encyclopedia.* [Online] Cloverleaf Farm, LLC, 2014. http://www.cloverleaffarmherbs.com/rhatany/#sthash.kLqBzUy4.dpbs.

148. [Online] Pratt, Keith L.; Richard Rutt, James Hoare (1999). Korea: a historical and cultural dictionary. Richmond, Surrey.: Curzon Press. pp. pp. 310–310. ISBN 0-7007-0464-7..

149. [Online] Vergano, D. Herbal 'remedy' may trigger widespread kidney failure. USA Today April 16, 2012..

150. [Online] http://montana.plant-life.org/species/erod_cicu.htm.

151. Duke, James A. Helianthus annuus. *Purdue University.* [Online] Center for New Crops & Plants Products, January 7, 1998. https://www.hort.purdue.edu/newcrop/duke_energy/Helianthus_annuus.html.

152. Kress, Henriette. Melilotus. *Henriette's Herbal.* [Online] 2014. http://www.henriettes-herb.com/eclectic/kings/melilotus.html.

153. [Online] http://nativequotesandbrilliance.ning.com/profiles/blogs/plants-indian-paintbrush-a-k-a-castilleja-or-prairie-fire.

154. Grieve, M. Ash, Wafer. *Botanical.com.* [Online] 2014. https://www.botanical.com/botanical/mgmh/a/ashwa078.html.

155. Dudnic, Natalia. The prospect of using an extract of Juglans regia in the prevention of iodine deficiency diseases. *National Council*

for Accreditation and Attestation. [Online] December 17, 2009. http://www.cnaa.acad.md/en/thesis/14264/.

156. Uphof, J. C. Th. *Dictionary of Economic Plants.* s.l. : H.R. Engelmann (J. Cramer), 1959.

157. Dow, Elaine. A Short History of Dye Plants. *The New England Unit of The Herb Society of America.* [Online] January 2, 2008. http://www.neuhsa.org/dyeplant-history.html.

158. Horne, S., Perretty, P. Oats. *Tree of Light.* [Online] 2008. http://www.treelite.com/NF/2008/07/Oats-Avena-sativa.

159. McDonald, Jim. Michigan Midwive's Association Spring Conference 2010 Notes on Classes by Herbalist Jim McDonald. *Herbcraft.* [Online] June 4, 2012. http://www.herbcraft.org/MMA.pdf.

160. Kindscher, Kelly. *Medicinal Wild Plants of the Prairie.* Lawrence : University Press of Kansas, 1992.

161. Scooter Cheatham, and Marshall Johnston, and Lynn Marshall. *The Useful Wild Plants of Texas, the Southeastern and Southwestern United States, the Southern Plains, and Northern Mexico VOLUME 2.* s.l. : Useful Wild Plants Inc., 1995.

162. Telkes, Nicole. *Personal Experience.*

163. Knishinsky, R. *Prickly Pear Cactus Medicine: Treatments for Diabetes, Cholesterol, and the Immune System.* s.l. : Healing Arts Press, 2004.

164. A Navarrete, F Palacios-Espinosa , R Mata. Gastroprotective Effect of Brickellia cavanillesii (Cav) B. L. Robinson (Asteraceae).... *Thieme, Planta Medica.* [Online] 2011. https://www.thieme-connect.com/ejournals/abstract/10.1055/s-0031-1273581.

165. Karl-Heinz A. Rosler, Robert S. Goodwin , Tom J. Mabry , Shambhu D. Varma , John Norris. Flavonoids with Anti-Cataract

Activity from Brickellia arguta. *Journal of Natural Products.*
[Online] http://pubs.acs.org/doi/abs/10.1021/np50032a014.

INDEX

193

194

195

196

Made in the USA
Coppell, TX
08 January 2023

10656296R10119